The Edible Wild Plants Bible

[7 In 1] The All-In-One Guide to Identifying, Harvesting, Foraging and Cooking Edible Wild Plants Without Fear | Colorful Edition

Wilson Parker

TABLE OF CONTENTS

INTRODUCTION

The world of edible wild plants is still mostly uncharted territory for many of us. We have lost touch with our ancestors' understanding of the natural world and the wealth it offers in an age where convenience and rapid gratification are prioritized over all other considerations. However, knowing about and consuming wild plants has many benefits because they are nutritious, long-lasting, and even tasty. They also strengthen our connection to the land and our respect for the natural world and its complex web of life. Nothing else can do this.

The goal of this book, "The Complete Guide to Locating, Identifying, Harvesting and Preparing Edible Wild Plants," is to provide readers with a thorough introduction to the world of edible wild plants. This book is the ideal resource for anybody wishing to get in touch with the land and its abundance, covering everything from the fundamentals of foraging to the latest cutting-edge methods for recognizing and cooking wild plants. This book has something for everyone, whether you are an experienced forager or a novice who is just inquisitive.

The basis for successful foraging is laid out in this book. It discusses the fundamentals of foraging, including safety precautions, ethical issues surrounding wild gathering, and the tools and gear required for a fruitful foraging expedition. The several habitats that wild plants can be found in will be covered in this book, and readers will learn how to recognize these areas to increase their chances of success. This section also offers a summary of the various edible plant species that can be discovered in the wild, ranging from fruits and nuts to roots and shoots.

Additionally, this book is devoted to identifying wild plants that are edible. It discusses the essential qualities that set edible plants apart from their non-edible cousins, such as their physical traits, morphology, and environmental conditions. Readers will learn how to recognize a variety of wild plants that are edible, from well-known species like dandelion and wild garlic to less well-known species like wild ginger and chanterelle mushrooms.

It also covers the practical side of foraging, such as how to gather and cook wild plants. The best time and location to harvest each plant will be identified, and readers will learn how to use a variety of methods to guarantee a plentiful harvest. The fundamentals of plant preparation, including cleaning, cooking, and preserving methods, are also covered in this section. Additionally, readers will discover how to prepare tasty and nourishing meals utilizing wild plants, ranging from straightforward salads to elaborate fares like soups and stews.

The last section of this book is devoted to sophisticated foraging methods. This section covers a wide range of subjects, including foraging in harsh areas like the Arctic and deserts as well as the use of wild plants for medicine. The use of GPS systems, botanical keys, and ethnobotanical expertise are just a few of the many methods and technologies that can be utilized to identify and gather wild plants.

For those prepared to invest the time to learn about the world of edible wild plants, the rewards are numerous. Wild plants not only provide a wholesome and sustainable source of nutrition, but they also profoundly bind us to the natural world. "The Complete Guide to Locating, Identifying, Harvesting and Preparing Edible Wild Plants" is a priceless tool that will heighten your appreciation for the abundance of the natural world and the many gifts it has to offer, whether you are an experienced forager or a curious novice.

BOOK 1: THE BASICS OF FORAGING

CHAPTER ONE
THE MEANING OF WILD FOOD
*

Any plant, fungus, or animal that is collected, hunted, or caught from a non-domesticated environment, such as forests, meadows, streams, or even urban areas, is referred to as wild food. It can consist of anything from fish, game animals, and wild-caught seafood to wild berries and plants.

The term "wild food" frequently refers to the activity of "foraging," which entails looking for and gathering food in the wild. Foraging is a behavior that has been used by humans for thousands of years and is widespread across many civilizations. As individuals explore more environmentally friendly and wholesome food options as well as ways to get in touch with nature and the environment, there has been an increase in interest in foraging and wild food in recent years.

The natural nature of wild food is one of its defining qualities. In terms of flavor, texture, and nutritional value, it frequently differs from its domesticated cousins. For instance, because they evolved to the particular environmental conditions in which they develop, wild berries are frequently tastier and nutrient-dense than produced types. Unlike developed crops and domesticated animals, wild food is not subject to human alteration or intervention.

Because wild food is often only harvested seasonally and in small amounts, it is a more sustainable food source than industrial agriculture or animal husbandry. Wild food is less likely to be impacted by pesticides, herbicides, and other chemicals used in contemporary agriculture since it does not undergo the same level of human interference as cultivated crops.

Food from the wild is not just restricted to plants. A valuable supply of protein, good fats, and other nutrients not normally available in plant-based meals can be found through hunting and fishing. Especially in rural areas, hunting and fishing for wild animals and seafood are common activities.

Wild food occasionally has therapeutic advantages. For generations, many wild plants and fungi have been utilized in traditional medicine to treat a wide range of conditions, from minor illnesses to serious diseases. As an illustration, echinacea is frequently used as a natural cold and flu cure, and Chaga mushrooms are thought to have anti-inflammatory and anti-cancer qualities.

But it's important to understand that not all wild food is secure. Incorrect hunting and fishing techniques can be deadly, and some plants and fungus are poisonous or toxic. It is crucial to be fully knowledgeable about the local animals, plants, and fungi as well as the abilities and equipment required to gather them in an ethical and safe manner.

In recent years, gourmet culinary items made from wild food have grown in appeal. Chefs and food lovers have begun incorporating wild foodstuffs into their menus to create dishes that highlight the distinct flavors and textures of wild foods. But this pattern has also sparked worries about overharvesting and the effects of commercial harvesting on populations of wild food. To guarantee that these resources are accessible to future generations, it is crucial to harvest wild food in an ethical and sustainable manner.

In conclusion, any plant, fungus, or animal that has been foraged, hunted, or fished from a non-domesticated environment is referred to as wild food. Foraging is frequently connected to wild food, which is normally collected in seasonal modest amounts. Compared to industrial agriculture or animal husbandry, it is a more sustainable and diverse food source that can also offer important health and nutritional advantages. To collect wild food responsibly and sustainably, you must have a deep understanding of the plants, fungus, and animals in your area.

CHAPTER TWO

BENEFITS OF CONSUMING EDIBLE WILD PLANTS
*

For people throughout history, wild edible plants have been a vital source of both food and medicine. They are abundant in vitamins, minerals, antioxidants, and other useful elements that can enhance well-being and fend off disease. This post will discuss the several advantages of eating wild edible plants.

Nutritional Value: Compared to their produced equivalents, wild edible plants are frequently higher in nutrients. They can have higher levels of vitamins, minerals, and other healthy substances since they have evolved to adapt to their particular habitats. For instance, compared to cultivated versions, wild berries are frequently higher in vitamin C, antioxidants, and other minerals. Iron, calcium, and vitamin A are among the vitamins and minerals that are abundant in wild greens like dandelion and lamb quarters.

Wild edible plants are also abundant in antioxidants, which shield cells from damage brought on by free radicals. Free radicals are unsteady molecules that have the potential to harm cells and play a role in the onset of chronic illnesses like cancer, heart disease, and Alzheimer's disease. By scavenging free radicals, antioxidants lower the possibility of disease and cellular damage. A variety of wild plants, such as berries, herbs, and mushrooms, are beneficial complements to a healthy diet since they are high in antioxidants.

Many edible wild plants also have anti-inflammatory qualities in addition to their antioxidant properties. Numerous chronic diseases, such as arthritis, diabetes, and heart disease, all include persistent inflammation. Consuming foods that are anti-inflammatory can help reduce inflammation, improving general health and lowering the risk of developing chronic diseases. Numerous natural plants have been found to have anti-inflammatory qualities, such as ginger, turmeric, and wild berries.

Digestive Health: Edible plants found in the wild can also aid with digestive health. Many wild greens, like dandelion and chicory, are bitter, encouraging healthy digestion by triggering the creation of digestive fluids and enzymes. Additionally, a variety of natural plants, such as yarrow and wild mint, have been traditionally utilized to treat digestive issues and as digestive aids.

Support for the Immune System: Wild edible plants can also help the immune system. Elderberries, rose hips, and echinacea are just a few examples of the many wild plants that are abundant in vitamins and antioxidants that boost the immune system and guard against illness and disease. Additionally, many wild plants, including ginger and garlic, contain antibacterial qualities that aid in the prevention of infections and enhance immune function.

Wild edible plants can also be beneficial for one's mental health. Numerous flora, such as lavender, chamomile, and St. John's wort, has been used for centuries to treat anxiety, depression, and other mood disorders. Additionally, spending time outdoors and gathering wild herbs can have a relaxing and centered effect that helps to promote general wellbeing and lower stress.

Eating edible plants from the wild helps to encourage ethical and sustainable eating. Foraging for wild plants is a sustainable, low-impact alternative to industrial agriculture and animal husbandry as a means of acquiring sustenance. By consuming wild plants, we can benefit regional ecosystems and lessen our dependency on industrial agriculture. In addition, gathering wild plants can encourage a closer relationship with the natural world and the ecosystem, which can help us be more conscientious about the influence of the foods we eat on the environment.

A number of wild food plants have cultural importance as well. Wild plants are a vital component of the food and cultural history of many indigenous peoples and traditional societies. Eating wild plants can aid in the preservation of traditional knowledge and cultural traditions, fostering diversity and honoring the long history and diversity of human culture.

Finally, for their nutritional value and health advantages, wild edible plants are a useful resource. They are a great source of minerals, anti-oxidants, and other healthy substances that can improve general health and lower the risk of chronic illnesses. Consuming a diet high in wild plants can boost the immune system, digestive system, and mental health. It can also lower inflammation. Eating wild plants can also help regional ecosystems, encourage ethical eating, and lessen our dependency on industrial agriculture.

A rewarding and enjoyable hobby is foraging for wild food plants. It inspires us to spend more time outside and have a greater understanding of and respect for nature. Finding wild plants when foraging can be a terrific way to get to know the locals and discover their customs and foodways.

Foraging must be done responsibly and in harmony with the ecosystem, though. Before consuming any plants, it's crucial to become familiar with your local flora and be confident in your ability to recognize them. If not properly identified and processed, several wild plants might be poisonous or hazardous. Furthermore, it is crucial to forage sustainably by taking only what you require and leaving enough for the plant to recover and for other animals to eat.

In conclusion, wild edible plants are a sustainable and moral source of food that have a variety of health advantages. More wild plants in our diet can improve our general health and wellbeing, foster a connection to nature, and advance environmental sustainability.

CHAPTER THREE

UNDERSTANDING FORAGING
*

Gathering wild edible plants, mushrooms, and other food sources from the environment is known as foraging. Humans have been engaging in this activity for countless years, and for many people today it is still the primary source of sustenance. This essay will examine the relevance and meaning of foraging, its background, and its place in contemporary society. Gathering wild food from the outdoors is a practice known as foraging. Wild vegetation such as berries, nuts, roots, mushrooms, wild game, and fish can be included in this list of supplies. There are many different types of foraging, from picking wild berries while hiking to hunting and fishing for large game. Food can be found ethically and sustainably by foraging. Foraging has a lower environmental impact than industrial agriculture and animal husbandry because it doesn't involve the use of pesticides, fertilizers, or other chemicals. Additionally, foraging encourages a closer relationship with the natural world and can build a sense of community and shared environmental responsibility.

Human culture has included foraging for thousands of years. Up until the introduction of agriculture, foraging was the major method of collecting food for early people, and it continued to be a crucial source of sustenance. Foraging was nevertheless a vital aspect of many communities even after agriculture had been developed, especially in places where it was difficult or impossible to practice agriculture.

Around the world, many traditional civilizations have acquired highly developed foraging techniques and in-depth knowledge of the environment and available resources. Native Americans in North America, for instance, have typically relied on hunting, fishing, and harvesting wild herbs to survive. They have a profound grasp of the natural world, its cycles, and the intricate spiritual and cultural traditions associated with gathering and utilizing the environment.

In today's culture, foraging is crucial, especially in rural and isolated locations where access to supermarkets and other food sources may be limited. For instance, many Alaskan tribes rely on foraging, gathering berries, wild game, and fish all year long for livelihood.

Urban regions have seen a rise in the popularity of foraging as residents look for more ethical and environmentally friendly ways to get their food. Foraging may be a gratifying and enjoyable pastime that inspires individuals to spend more time outside and gain a better appreciation of nature.

Foraging in metropolitan places can be difficult, though, because the human activity may harm and degrade the environment. Urban foraging requires extreme caution and awareness of potential dangers including tainted water sources and toxic air.

Plant foraging, mushroom foraging, berry foraging, and nut foraging are a few examples of foraging. Each kind of foraging has its own set of knowledge and skill requirements as well as distinct nutritional advantages.

Plant foraging is the process of identifying and gathering wild plants for nourishment. There are edible plants in a variety of settings, including wetlands, fields, and forests. For safe and effective foraging, the ability to identify plants is essential because many plants might be hazardous or inedible. Some wild plants are even more nutrient-dense than domesticated crops, including in terms of vitamins, minerals, and antioxidants. For instance, spinach lacks the iron and calcium that wild greens like dandelion and chickweed do.

The act of gathering wild mushrooms for nourishment is known as mushroom foraging. Forests, meadows, and wetlands are just a few of the several settings where mushrooms can be found. They may make a delightful meal addition and are a great source of protein, fiber, and vitamins. But finding mushrooms demands a high level of expertise and understanding because some of them can be poisonous or even fatal. Even seasoned foragers might make blunders when trying to identify a mushroom. Before attempting to forage mushrooms, it is crucial to obtain advice from seasoned foragers or complete a course.

Berry foraging, or gathering wild berries like blueberries, raspberries, and blackberries, is done for food. Berries can be consumed fresh or frozen for later consumption and are high in vitamins, antioxidants, and fiber. Berry foraging is rather simple because many berries are simple to identify and are present in a variety of settings, including fields, forests, and cities. However, it is critical to be mindful of any potential hazards associated with picking berries, such as coming into contact with poison ivy or ticks.

The act of gathering wild nuts for food, such as acorns, chestnuts, and hickory nuts, is known as nut foraging. Nuts can be consumed raw or roasted and are a wonderful source of protein, vitamins, and beneficial fats. Understanding the many varieties of nuts and the environments in which they thrive is necessary for nut foraging. For instance, before acorns, which are found in oak woodlands, can be eaten, they must undergo special processing to get rid of the bitter tannins.

Foraging Morality

It is important to approach foraging with respect for the ecosystem and its resources. Foraging sustainably is only taking what is necessary, leaving enough for the plant or animal to regenerate, and allowing enough for other animals to eat.

It is also necessary for ethical foraging, which respects the rights of other users of the land as well as the environment. For instance, it is imperative to get the go-ahead from landowners before foraging on private property and to stay away from foraging in designated or protected areas.

Although foraging can be enjoyable and rewarding, it is important to proceed with caution and be aware of any potential risks. If not properly identified and prepared, several wild plants and mushrooms might be poisonous or deadly. It's crucial to become knowledgeable about the local plants and mushrooms in your area and to be able to reliably identify them before ingesting them.

It is imperative to stay away from regions that have been treated with pesticides or other chemicals when foraging for wild plants. The plants must be adequately cleaned and prepared in order to get rid of any dirt, insects, or other impurities.

For instance, trekking, climbing, or other physically demanding activities can make foraging physically taxing. Being physically fit and taking the necessary measures, like packing enough water and donning the proper gear and footwear, are vital.

The act of obtaining wild edible plants, mushrooms, and other food sources from the environment is known as foraging. Humans have used this sustainable and moral method of collecting food for thousands of years. Foraging can encourage a closer bond with nature, build a feeling of community, and offer a nutrient-rich source of food as well as other advantageous ingredients. Foraging should be done responsibly, though, and the ecosystem should be respected. Foraging must be done sustainably, ethically, and while being aware of potential dangers and safety measures. We may keep taking use of the many advantages of this age-old tradition while preserving the natural world for future generations by foraging wisely.

Because it has so many advantages, foraging is a favorite pastime for plenty of people all around the world. The following are some justifications for foraging:

Nature connection: Foraging enables people to make a connection with nature that is not achievable through other hobbies. Foragers can gain a deeper understanding and appreciation of the natural world by spending time in natural settings and learning about the plants and animals that inhabit them.

Sustainability: Since foraging relies on the growth and reproduction of plants and animals naturally, it is a sustainable method of obtaining food. Foraging, when done properly, can help foster a more sustainable food system by reducing reliance on industrial agriculture.

Nutrition: Due to their higher concentration of advantageous chemicals, wild edible plants and mushrooms are frequently more nutrient-dense than their produced counterparts. A wide variety of foods rich in vitamins, minerals, and other nutrients are available to foragers.

Diversity: People can sample a greater variety of meals by foraging than they might in a grocery store or restaurant. By eating new foods and experimenting with various preparations, foragers can broaden their culinary horizons and cultivate a more diverse palette.

Saving money on food is possible through foraging because it reduces the need to buy pricey specialty foods. Many edible plants and mushrooms are thriving in local surroundings, frequently for no cost to foragers.

Building a community: Foraging is a common social activity that can bring individuals together to exchange information and resources. Foragers might meet people who share their interests and values by taking part in regional foraging clubs or activities.

Overall, foraging provides a special and satisfying way to interact with nature and find wholesome, sustainable nourishment. Everyone of any age or background may enjoy it, and it is a great approach to encourage a closer relationship with the environment and our food.

FORAGING VS WILD FOOD
*

Although they are frequently used synonymously, foraging and wild food are not the same. Wild food is defined as coming from sources that are not domesticated, whereas foraging refers to acquiring food from the natural world. Although not all wild food is obtained by foraging, it is a sort of collecting in this sense.

Foraged food has a lower nutritional value than wild food, depending on a number of variables. Consider these significant variations:

Diversity: Compared to non-foragers, foragers have access to a broader selection of wild edible plants, mushrooms, and other edibles. This is due to the fact that foragers frequently have a greater understanding of the local ecosystem and the various types of food that are present there. By exploring various habitats and seasons, foragers can find wild foods that are rich in nutrients and other helpful components.

Seasonality: Foragers frequently depend on wild foods' seasonal availability, which might have an impact on their nutritional content. Depending on when they are gathered, some wild edible plants and mushrooms are only available at specific seasons of the year and have varying nutrient contents. For instance, certain wild plants may contain more vitamins and minerals when they initially bloom in the early spring, but others may contain more nutrients when they are getting ready to go dormant for the winter.

Soil quality: The nutritional content of wild food might vary depending on the quality of the soil in which it is cultivated. Wild foods can have more vitamins, minerals, and other useful components when grown on soils rich in nutrients and organic matter. However, wild foods that are grown on soils tainted with pollutants or heavy metals may be less nutrient-dense and even dangerous to consume.

Food produced in the wild may have a different nutritional value. For instance, some edible wild plants and mushrooms could require cooking or processing to get rid of toxins or increase digestibility. Additionally, certain cooking techniques, including drying, fermenting, or pickling, can maintain or improve the nutritional value of wild foods.

environmental elements Finally, many environmental elements including climate, altitude, and sunshine exposure might have an impact on the nutritional value of wild food. These elements may have an impact on the nutritional makeup of wild plants and animals by affecting their growth and development.

Overall, foraged and wild foods can be very nutrient-dense and offer a number of health advantages. However, with the right information and caution, foraged and wild foods can contribute to a balanced, healthful diet. But while gathering and consuming wild food, it's crucial to proceed with caution and take the proper safety precautions. Furthermore, it's critical to be aware of the dangers associated with consuming wild food that has been tainted with pollution or other dangerous elements.

In addition to the nutritional differences noted above, the following are other distinctions between foraged and wild foods:

Definition: The act of looking for and obtaining wild foods and other resources from the natural environment is known as foraging. Contrarily, the term "wild food" refers specifically to edible plants and animals that can be found in the wild.

With intention, foraging is the deliberate pursuit of wild foods for dietary, medicinal, or other uses. Contrarily, wild food can apply to any food that is discovered in the wild, regardless of whether it was purposefully sought out.

Diversity: Fruits and berries can be collected, wild game can be hunted, wild mushrooms can be harvested, and wild herbs can be harvested. On the other hand, when someone talks of "wild food," they typically mean just those plants and animals that can be found in the wild and are edible.

Context: Modern initiatives promoting sustainable living and regional food systems frequently link foraging with traditional or indigenous traditions. On the other hand, wild food can be employed in a variety of settings, such as survival situations, leisure activities like camping and hiking, and culinary arts.

Knowledge and skill are frequently needed for foraging in order to recognize and safely gather wild foods. The capacity to identify plants and animals, comprehend how seasonal and environmental factors affect food availability, and be aware of any risks or dangers that may come with eating wild foods are a few examples of this. On the other hand, eating wild food is possible without having the same amount of understanding or experience. Nevertheless, it is still crucial to use caution and adhere to fundamental food safety regulations.

Wild food and foraging are similar ideas, although they apply to slightly distinct things. The act of looking for and obtaining wild foods and other resources from the natural environment is referred to as foraging. On the other hand, wild food specifically refers to the plants and animals that can be consumed as food.

BOOK 2: GETTING STARTED WITH EDIBLE PLANTS

CHAPTER ONE

BEFORE YOU GO: GUIDELINES FOR FORAGING
*

The goal of foraging guidelines is to encourage ethical and sustainable collecting methods that safeguard the environment and the forager. Foragers can reduce their negative effects on the environment, prevent themselves from getting hurt, and guarantee that they pick edible plants in a safe and sustainable manner by adhering to these rules.

Making ensuring that foragers are aware of the potential environmental effects of their behavior is one of the main goals of foraging guidelines. Understanding the function of plants and animals in the environment as well as the possible effects of harvesting them is part of this. Foragers should be aware of local foraging laws and restrictions and show respect for both private property owners' and public land managers' rights.

Making sure that foragers are aware of the plants they are harvesting is a key aspect of foraging rules. Foragers should be able to distinguish between edible and harmful plants. The possible impacts of various harvesting methods on the plants and their habitats should also be known to them. For instance, over-harvesting or using the wrong equipment can harm the plant and its habitat, possibly restricting its accessibility to future foragers.

Ethical harvesting procedures are also covered in foraging guidelines. Foragers ought to use ethical harvesting practices, such as taking only what is required, avoiding vulnerable ecosystems, and having as little of an influence on wildlife as possible. They must also be conscious of how their behaviors can affect other foragers and the larger community.

Guidelines for foraging can assist safeguard the safety of the forager in addition to encouraging sustainable and ethical harvesting techniques. Foragers need to be mindful of hazardous plants, threatening creatures, and natural dangers like rocky terrain or steep slopes. Advice on how to prevent these risks and what to do when they are encountered can be found in the guidelines.

Foragers can make sure they are making responsible decisions that are advantageous to both themselves and the environment by adhering to foraging rules. They can safeguard themselves from potential threats while minimizing their influence on the ecosystem and the plant populations they are gathering. Responsible foraging techniques can also build a feeling of community among foragers, encourage the sharing of information and resources, and support long-term sustainable harvesting methods.

The promotion of ethical and sustainable harvesting techniques depends on foraging rules. By following these recommendations, foragers can reduce their negative effects on the ecosystem, securely and sustainably gather edible plants, and safeguard themselves from dangers.

The capacity of foragers to collaborate and advance moral, responsible, and sustainable gathering methods that are advantageous to both themselves and the environment is essential to the long-term survival of foraging practices.

Prior to leaving on a foraging expedition, it is crucial to be aware of what to anticipate and how to get ready. This chapter will discuss how crucial it is to be prepared before going foraging in the fields.

Foraging effectively requires an understanding of edible plant identification. Knowing the difference between edible and inedible plants, as well as which plants are dangerous and should be avoided, is crucial. Foragers can avoid unintentionally picking harmful or unpalatable plants by performing proper identification.

Foraging can only last as long as people are aware of the fundamentals of sustainability. Foragers need to be aware that excessive harvesting has a negative effect on plant populations and their environments. Foraging can be continued sustainably and morally by using proper harvesting methods, such as taking only what is required and avoiding vulnerable areas.

Having Ecosystem Knowledge as a Forager

Understanding your ecosystem as a forager is essential for establishing a secure, ethical, and sustainable activity. All live things and the non-living components of their surroundings are included in the ecosystem. The significance of understanding your ecosystem as a forager and how to do so will be discussed in this essay.

Knowing your ecology as a forager has many advantages, one of which is figuring out which plants and animals are suitable for consumption. Knowing the ecological interactions between various species, such as those between predators and prey, can help determine which plants and animals are most likely to be safe to eat. For instance, if you see birds eating a certain plant, it is probably safe for you to eat.

It can be easier to decide which species to avoid or only harvest in modest quantities if you are aware of the ecology of the area and the species that are present. Knowing your ecology can also aid you in recognizing rare or endangered flora and animals. These species must not be harvested since human activity and environmental factors are already having a negative impact on their populations.

Knowing your ecology is important because it helps a forager understand how human activity affects the environment. When carried out in a way that doesn't endanger the ecosystem or the species it supports, foraging can be a sustainable and moral activity. Overfishing, habitat damage, and pollution are all elements that can harm the ecology, though. You can establish sustainable harvesting procedures that reduce the environmental effect by being aware of the environmental constraints and challenges that your ecosystem is facing.

There are various actions you may take as a forager to gain a deeper grasp of your ecology. The first step is to learn about the ecology of the area you intend to forage in. Studying the local flora and fauna as well as the geological and climatic characteristics of the area might all fall under this category. The more you are familiar with the area where you will be foraging, the better equipped you will be to recognize the plants and animals you come across and comprehend the ecological relevance of what you are seeing.

Engaging with regional professionals and organizations is another method to increase your understanding of ecosystems. This may entail joining a neighborhood naturalist group or going to seminars and lectures given by authorities in the area. These groups can offer helpful advice, materials, and chances to interact with other foragers and gain knowledge from their experiences.

Additionally, spending time in the area itself is a beneficial approach to learning about ecology. You can develop a greater understanding of the intricacy and interconnection of the ecosystem by paying close attention to the interactions between plants and animals. Spending time outdoors can also help you learn to appreciate the richness and beauty of the natural world, which can further motivate you to engage in ethical and sustainable foraging techniques.

Foragers that want to engage in ethical, sustainable, and safe foraging must be familiar with their local ecosystem. Foragers can gain a better appreciation for nature and a clearer knowledge of their place in it by learning about the local flora and fauna, the effects of human activity on the ecosystem, and interacting with local experts and organizations. In the end, having this information can make foraging more enjoyable and meaningful while preserving the environment's health and vitality.

The Laws Associated with Foraging

Foraging can be enjoyable and rewarding, but it's important to understand the rules and laws that apply to it. These regulations are in place to safeguard the environment, the animals that live there, and the humans who use it. Here, we'll look at why it's crucial to understand foraging-related laws and how to keep up with them.

Avoiding legal problems is one of the main advantages of being aware of the regulations governing foraging. Foraging laws vary from place to region, therefore it's critical to understand what is and isn't acceptable. There are severe guidelines in some locations regarding what kinds of plants and animals can be collected and how much can be gathered. In other places, foraging may be completely outlawed.

For instance, the National Park Service in the United States maintains stringent rules on foraging in its parks. Unless specifically permitted by the superintendent, foraging is generally not permitted in national parks. By doing this, visitors can enjoy the parks' delicate ecosystems for many years to come.

Similar to the United States, foraging is typically permitted in the United Kingdom as long as it is done for personal consumption and not for profit. It's important to consult with local authorities first before taking any wild plants or animals, as there are certain exceptions to this generalization.

Understanding the regulations governing foraging can also prevent you from unintentionally taking endangered or protected species. Laws prohibiting the collection of specific plant and animal species are commonplace. These rules are in place to protect biodiversity and stop the extinction of certain species.

For instance, the European Union's Habitat Directive safeguards a number of plant and animal species throughout the continent, such as the wildcat, the otter, and various kinds of bats. It is prohibited to hunt, kill, or disturb any member of these species. This includes collecting any plants or fungi that might serve as the animals' habitat or food.

Making sure the plants and animals you collect are safe to consume is another crucial component of understanding the regulations governing foraging. It's crucial to appropriately identify any potentially harmful plants or fungus. Foragers must be able to identify the plants and fungi they are collecting, and they must take precautions to make sure they are not collecting any dangerous species, according to rules in many places.

For instance, the Food and Drug Administration (FDA) has rules that mandate foragers correctly identify mushrooms before selling them commercially in the United States. These laws were put in place to stop the sale of dangerous or even lethal poisonous mushrooms, which can be consumed.

So how do you stay up to date on the regulations governing foraging? Investigating the rules and legislation in your neighborhood is one option. You can do this by getting in touch with local government entities like state parks or departments of natural resources. The laws and restrictions governing foraging can frequently be found by contacting local foraging organizations or naturalist clubs.

Attending forage-related workshops or events is another approach to staying current on the regulations governing foraging. These gatherings frequently feature professionals who may offer advice on sustainable foraging techniques as well as knowledge of the local rules and ordinances.

Finally, when foraging, it's crucial to employ common sense. Always treat the environment and the wildlife in it with respect. To prevent injuring the environment or the species you are harvesting, use proper harvesting methods. Never take more than you need from any rare or endangered species.

To engage in safe, ethical, and sustainable foraging, it is crucial to understand the regulations governing this activity. You can stay out of trouble legally and make sure that your foraging techniques are sustainable and safe by being aware of the laws in your neighborhood and keeping up with them.

Choosing the Right Foods

The act of foraging involves looking for and obtaining wild food sources. It is a long-standing and fundamental practice in numerous civilizations all across the world. A strong connection to nature and a sustainable source of nutrition can both be found through foraging. Knowing how to recognize and locate the desired food is one of the fundamental components of foraging. Understanding the local environment is necessary for this, as well as the kinds of plants and animals that grow there or reside there, as well as their seasonal rhythms and habitats. It also calls for familiarity with the target food's appearance, flavor, and nutritional characteristics.

Fruits, berries, nuts, seeds, roots, tubers, mushrooms, and wild game are just a few of the target foods that foragers can be looking for. For each of these to successfully forage, specific skills and expertise are needed.

Foragers' favorite and most identifiable target foods are frequently fruits and berries. They typically have vibrant colors and a sweet or tangy flavor. They can be found in a variety of settings, including forests, meadows, and wetlands, and they may grow on trees, shrubs, or vines. Strawberries, blueberries, raspberries, blackberries, cherries, plums, and apples are a few examples of common wild fruits and berries.

Foragers may find nuts and seeds to be a good target food because of their high protein and fat content. Acorns, chestnuts, walnuts, hazelnuts, and sunflower seeds are a few common wild nuts and seeds. These can be discovered on shrubs, trees, or in the undergrowth of woodlands and forests.

Another crucial target food for foragers is roots and tubers. These may include a lot of carbohydrates and other nutrients, and they may also be therapeutic. Dandelion, burdock, wild carrots, and cattail tubers are examples of typical wild roots and tubers.

Many foragers prize mushrooms as a target food, but they can be harmful if not identified properly. Before attempting to forage for mushrooms, it is imperative to have a firm grasp of mushroom identification. Wild mushrooms come in a variety of common varieties, such as morels, chanterelles, boletes, and oysters.

Foragers can also use the wild game, such as deer, elk, rabbits, and birds, as a source of sustenance. However, compared to plant foraging, hunting and trapping need

distinct knowledge and tools. It is crucial to abide by all local hunting and trapping laws as well as to respect the prey species.

To properly locate and identify target foods, foragers need to have a thorough understanding of the surrounding ecosystem. Understanding the different kinds of plants and animals that grow there or inhabit it, as well as their seasonal rhythms and habitats, is part of this.

This information can also be acquired through experience and observation. Foragers can gain a thorough grasp of their surroundings by spending time outdoors and observing the plants and animals that are present. Additionally, they can pick up tips from knowledgeable locals and elders who have been foraging in the area for years.

The local environment can also be learned about through study and investigation. There are several resources that can give knowledge on local flora and wildlife, including field guides, books, internet forums, and courses. Cross-referencing information from many sources is crucial, and false information must be avoided.

Foragers must be aware of any potential threats or hazards in addition to knowing the food they are looking for. This could include hazardous animals, poisonous plants, or contaminated habitats. When foraging in a new area, it is crucial to exercise caution and always err on the side of safety.

Once the desired food has been discovered, foragers must think about how to ethically and sustainably get it. The ecosystem's long-term health and the survival of the foraging culture depend on the ethical and sustainable harvesting of target food. Foragers can ensure that they are gathering sustainably and ethically by adhering to a number of guidelines. The first rule is to only take what is necessary. Foragers should limit their harvest to what they will really consume and refrain from overharvesting or taking more than the ecology can support. This makes it more likely that there will be enough target food for current and future generations, as well as for dependent species.

The second rule is to harvest with as little harm to the environment as possible. Foragers should refrain from disturbing the soil or trampling on other plants when collecting roots or tubers, for instance. When gathering fruits or nuts, they should also take care not to harm the bark of trees or plants.

Respecting the ecosystem's natural balance is the third guiding concept. Avoiding the removal of entire plants or the alteration of vital habitats for other species entails doing this. Foragers should also refrain from gathering their intended food in protected areas or regions that are crucial to the survival of threatened or endangered species.

The fourth rule is to refrain from spreading infectious diseases or invading species to new places. The movement of seeds, spores, or other organisms from one environment to another should be avoided by foragers. The potential dangers of introducing new species or illnesses to an environment should also be understood by them, and they should take efforts to prevent doing so.

The fifth rule is to use morally responsible harvesting methods. For instance, before harvesting on private property, foragers must always obtain permission from the owners. Additionally, they should observe any cultural or spiritual traditions that pertain to food gathering and targeting.

Foragers should be mindful of the potential effects of climate change on the distribution and availability of target food in addition to these guidelines. The development and dispersion of plants and animals can be impacted by changes in temperature, precipitation, and weather patterns, necessitating modifications to foraging strategies or target food selections.

Knowing your target food as a forager necessitates a thorough comprehension of the surrounding ecosystem, the target food, and ethical and sustainable harvesting practices. Foragers can contribute to ensuring the continuous availability of the target food for future generations by adhering to these guidelines and maintaining the ecosystem's natural equilibrium.

Understanding Wild Plants Habitat

The physical and biological contexts in which living things interact with one another and their surroundings are referred to as habitats and ecosystems. They can range in size from tiny dirt patches to full biomes that span vast stretches of land. The various ecosystems and habitat types, as well as their characteristics and the kinds of plants and animals that live there, will all be covered in this article.

Earth's Ecosystems: Land-based ecosystems are referred to as terrestrial ecosystems, and there are six different types of terrestrial ecosystems: tropical rainforests, temperate forests, grasslands, deserts, tundra, and taiga.

Tropical rainforests are found close to the equator and are distinguished by hot, muggy weather and a lot of rain. Primates, insects, and reptiles are just a few of the many plants and creatures that may be found in these forests due to the dense flora.

In areas with a moderate climate and lots of rainfall, like the eastern United States and parts of Europe and Asia, temperate forests can be found. Deciduous trees, which lose their leaves in the fall, and coniferous trees, which are evergreens, are the main features of these woods. Many different species of animals, such as bears, deer, and migratory birds, can be found in temperate forests.

Tall grasses and a lack of trees are characteristics of grasslands. They can be found all over the world in regions with average rainfall, including the Midwest of the United States and African savannas. Numerous grazing species, including bison and antelope, as well as predators like lions and hyenas, can be found in grasslands.

Deserts are regions with relatively little rainfall and are distinguished by their high temperatures and dry weather. Many plant and animal species, including cacti, reptiles, and insects, have adapted to survive in the desert despite its harsh environment.

Alaska and Siberia are examples of areas close to the North Pole that have tundra, a frigid, treeless habitat. A distinctive ecosystem of plants and animals, including caribou, arctic foxes, and polar bears, is supported by the frozen ground in these areas.

The taiga biome, commonly referred to as the boreal forest, is found in northern regions of the world like Canada, Scandinavia, and Russia and is distinguished by coniferous forests. Numerous species of animals, such as moose, wolves, and bears, can be found in the taiga.

Ecosystems in Water

Ecosystems found in bodies of water, such as lakes, rivers, oceans, and wetlands, are referred to as aquatic ecosystems. These habitats can be further divided into freshwater and marine environments.

In water bodies with little salt content, like lakes, ponds, and rivers, freshwater ecosystems can be found. These environments can support a wide variety of plant and animal species, including fish, amphibians, and aquatic plants. They are distinguished by their flowing or still water.

Oceanic ecosystems, which make up more than 70% of the Earth's surface, are referred to as marine ecosystems. These ecosystems comprise a variety of habitats, such as coral reefs, open oceans, and estuaries, and are distinguished by their high salinity levels. Whales, dolphins, and sharks are just a few of the many plant and animal species that may be found in marine ecosystems.

Wet soils and shallow water tables are two characteristics that distinguish wetlands as distinct habitats. Both freshwater and saltwater ecosystems have them, and they are home to a wide variety of plant and animal species, such as waterfowl, beavers, and cattails.

There are many different types of habitats and ecosystems, and each one has distinctive qualities that sustain a wide variety of plant and animal life. The sustainable use of natural resources and conservation efforts both depend on an understanding of the many ecosystems and habitat types. By defending these ecosystems and preserving their biodiversity, we can ensure the health and well-being of both humans and the planet as a whole. It is important to note that these ecosystems are not static and are constantly changing due to natural processes and human activities, such as climate change, deforestation, and pollution. As such, it is crucial that we work towards preserving and restoring these ecosystems for future generations.

The role of Soil, Water, and Climate

Our planet's ecosystems depend critically on the health of the soil, water, and climate systems. This article will examine the distinct functions of soil, water, and climate as well as how they work together to sustain life on Earth.

Soil

In terrestrial ecosystems, the soil is an essential element that supports plant growth. It took thousands of years for the complex mixture of minerals, organic material, air, and water to form. In the ecosystem, soil serves a number of significant roles, including:

Nutrient Cycling: The nutrients that plants require to flourish, like nitrogen, phosphorus, and potassium, are stored in the soil. These nutrients are released back into the earth as plants grow and die, where other plants can repurpose them.

Water Storage: Soil absorbs rainwater and stores it so that plants can utilize it later. Agriculture systems don't need as much irrigation because healthy soil can hold onto water for extended periods of time.

Habitat: A wide variety of species that are crucial to the cycling of nutrients and decomposition, such as bacteria, fungus, and insects, can be found in soil.

However, the soil is a finite resource and is susceptible to deterioration as a result of human activities like agriculture, urbanization, and deforestation. Reduced agriculture yields, increased water pollution, and biodiversity loss can all be caused by degrading soil. In order to keep ecosystems healthy, it is crucial to protect and conserve soil health.

Water

All life on Earth depends on water, and ecosystem health depends on both its availability and quality. In the ecosystem, water serves a number of significant roles, including:

-   Water transports nutrients from the soil to plants and animals as they flow through the ecosystem.
-   Fish, amphibians, and insects, among other aquatic species, can all be found in water, which also serves as their habitat.
-   Water affects local and global temperature trends by absorbing and releasing heat energy, which contributes to climate regulation.
-   Water, like soil, is a finite resource that can degrade as a result of human activities like pollution and climate change. Climate change can affect water supply and quality, while water pollution can result in the extinction of aquatic life and impact human health. In order to preserve healthy ecosystems, it is crucial to safeguard and conserve water supplies.

Climate

The long-term trends of temperature, precipitation, and weather in a specific area are referred to as the climate. In the ecosystem, climate plays a number of significant roles, including:

-   Habitat: The kinds of plants and animals that can dwell in a certain area depending on the climate.
-   Climate has an impact on the rate of decomposition, the availability of nutrients, and plant development.
-   Ecosystem Services: Climate has an impact on the provision of ecosystem services that support human well-being, such as carbon sequestration.

Climate, however, is not a constant component and is susceptible to change as a result of both natural and man-made factors. Climate change has the potential to modify how ecosystems function, changing things like the distribution of species, phenology, and nutrient cycle. In order to preserve healthy ecosystems, it is crucial to reduce the effects of climate change and support ecosystem resilience.

Interactions

Climate, water availability, and soil composition are interrelated elements that affect how well ecosystems function. For instance, alterations in precipitation patterns due to climate change may affect how much water is available to both plants and animals. Water quality can also be impacted by soil health because healthy soil can filter contaminants before they reach rivers. Changes in water availability can also have an impact on soil-supported plant growth and nutrient cycling.

Soil, water, and climatic interactions must therefore be taken into account while managing ecosystems. Ecosystem functioning and the supply of ecosystem services that support human well-being can be supported through conservation activities that prioritize soil health, water quality, and climate resilience. Conservation agriculture and agroforestry are examples of sustainable land management techniques that can protect healthy soil and water supplies while lowering greenhouse gas emissions.

Finally, it should be noted that soil, water, and climate are all interrelated and crucial to the health and efficiency of ecosystems. Water is necessary for all life, the soil is the basis for plant growth, and climate affects how well ecosystems work and how well they can supply ecosystem services. These elements are susceptible to degradation as a result of human activities including pollution, deforestation, and climate change, which can impair ecosystem services, biodiversity, and human health. To sustain healthy ecosystems and the welfare of both humans and the earth, it is crucial to safeguard and conserve soil, water, and climatic resources.

Identifying wild plants by their preferred habitat

Foragers and environment lovers may find it helpful to identify wild plants based on their preferred habitat. In particular environmental conditions, such as soil type, sunlight exposure, and moisture levels, plants have evolved to thrive. You can focus your search and raise your chances of finding edible and medicinal plants by being aware of the environmental preferences of wild plants.

Following are some typical plant habitats and the kinds of plants that can be found there:

- Tall trees and a thick canopy that blocks sunlight are features of forests. The leaf litter and frequently shadowed forest floor create a moist and nutrient-rich habitat. Typical plants that you could discover in woodlands include:
- Wild garlic (Allium vineale) is a tough plant that thrives in damp, shady environments. It can be used as a flavoring or medicinal herb and has a powerful garlic aroma.
- Wild berries (Rubus spp.) flourish in forests, including blackberries, raspberries, and other berries. They can be picked in the late summer or early fall because they grow on shrubs.
- Wildflowers known as "goldenrod" (Solidago spp.) occur in forest clearings and along the edges of forests. Goldenrod is a vibrant yellow flower. It is used to treat respiratory and urinary tract infections in conventional medicine.

Meadows

Meadows are grassy places that frequently feature wildflowers and rolling hills. They receive a lot of sunshine and are typically nutrient-rich since there is plant matter that is degrading there. Meadows frequently contain the following kinds of plants:

- Wildflowers called milkweed (Asclepias spp.) bloom in meadows and other open spaces. It can be used in conventional medicine to treat respiratory issues and serves as the host plant for monarch butterfly caterpillars.
- The medicinal plant yarrow, or Achillea millefolium, is found in meadows and other open spaces. It contains tiny white blossoms and can be used to cure fever, wounds, and stomach problems.
- Hypericum perforatum, also known as St. John's Wort, is a medicinal plant that thrives in meadows and other open spaces. It can be used to relieve anxiety and despair and has yellow blossoms.

Wetlands

- Swamps, marshes, and bogs are examples of wetlands—areas that are heavily saturated with water. Standing water and a diversity of aquatic and semi-aquatic plants are frequently features that define them. Typical plants that can be discovered in wetlands include:
- Cattails (Typha spp.) is a semi-aquatic plant that can be found in marshes, by streams and ponds, and in other damp areas. They can be used to manufacture flour and other food products and are edible.
- Caltha palustris, sometimes known as the marsh marigold, is a vibrant yellow wildflower that thrives in wetlands and other moist environments. It is used in conventional medicine to treat a number of illnesses, such as joint pain and headaches.
- Horsetail (Equisetum spp.) is a perennial plant that originated in swamps and other moist environments. It has a lot of silica and can be used to fortify bones, hair, and nails.

Deserts

Deserts are arid areas with little or no rainfall. They frequently have minimal vegetation and sandy soil. Deserts often have a variety of flora, including:

- The prickly pear cactus (Opuntia spp.) is a succulent plant that thrives in arid climates like deserts. Its fruit can be used to produce jelly and other food products and is edible.
- Large, prickly shrubs known as Joshua trees (Yucca brevifolia) flourish in the Mojave Desert. They can live for hundreds of years and have long been regarded as an emblem of the American Southwest.

It is significant to remember that some wild plants can thrive in a range of habitats while others do not have specific habitat requirements. A lot of edible and medicinal plants also flourish in disturbed regions like fields, roadside ditches, and vacant lots. Nevertheless, knowing the wild plants' preferred habitats can help you find them and identify them in their native habitat.

It's crucial to harvest plants responsibly and just take what you need when foraging for wild plants. Before consuming any plants, make sure to correctly identify them. If in doubt, seek advice from a professional or reference manual. We can preserve the advantages of wild plants for future generations if we respect the environment and the plants that thrive there.

Foraging in different seasons

As a result of the fact that various species follow distinctive growth patterns and life cycles, the availability of wild plants might shift dramatically from one season to the next. Foragers can improve their ability to plan their harvests and maintain a sustainable and abundant supply of wild foods and medicines by becoming more familiar with the plants that are available during each season.

Spring: Spring is a time of regeneration, and as temperatures begin to rise and daylight hours lengthen, many wild plants begin to emerge from their dormant states and begin growing again. The appearance of edible greens in the wild, such as dandelion (Taraxacum officinale), chickweed (Stellaria media), and wild onion (Allium canadense), is one of the earliest indicators that spring has arrived. Foragers can benefit from using these plants in their diet because they are typically rich in a variety of vitamins and minerals. The understory of the forest is where you will find other springtime delicacies such as ramps (Allium tricoccum), fiddlehead ferns (Osmunda spp.), and morel mushrooms (Morchella spp.).

Summer: Summer is a time of plenty, and it is during this season that many wild plants are at their most robust and healthy. There is an abundance of wild fruits and berries, including wild plums (Prunus americana) and pawpaws (Asimina triloba), as well as blueberries (Vaccinium spp.), blackberries (Rubus spp.), raspberries (Rubus idaeus), and blueberries (Vaccinium spp.). You can also find edible flowers throughout the summer, such as elderflower (Sambucus spp.), honeysuckle (Lonicera spp.), and violets (Viola spp.), which lend color and flavor to salads and desserts.

Autumn: Autumn is a period of transition, as the weather begins to change from warm to cool and the days become shorter. During the fall, several types of wild plants start the process of generating seeds and storing nutrients in their roots in preparation for winter. During this time of year, wild nuts and seeds of many different kinds, such as acorns (Quercus spp.), hickory nuts (Carya spp.), and black walnuts (Juglans nigra), can be found and gathered by those who enjoy foraging. Persimmons (Diospyros virginiana) and wild grapes (Vitis spp.), both of which are at their sweetest and most flavorful throughout the fall, are also at their optimum during this season.

Foragers face a difficult time of year during the winter because many plants have either gone dormant or perished all the way back to the ground. However, there are several types of plants that can still be harvested during this time of year, such as evergreen trees and bushes. Tea can be made from pine needles (Pinus spp.), and a flavorful and healthy broth can be made from the needles and twigs of spruce (Picea spp.), fir (Abies spp.), and other species of coniferous trees. The bark of some trees, such as the birch (Betula spp.) and the slippery elm (Ulmus rubra), can be dried and powdered for therapeutic use. These barks can be found by winter foragers.

In conclusion, knowing how to forage is a useful ability that can give a source of food that is both fresh and nourishing as well as a source of medication throughout the entire year. Foragers are able to make the most of their harvests and secure a sustainable supply of wild foods for years to come when they have a thorough awareness of the seasonal cycles that wild plants follow. As is the case with gathering any type of wild food, it is essential to correctly identify plants, stay away from harvesting in places that are polluted, and employ harvesting methods that are responsible in order to safeguard the ecosystem and the plants that live within it.

CHAPTER TWO

THE FORAGING AND HARVESTING GEAR

*

The tools and equipment used to collect wild plants, fungi, and other natural resources from the environment are referred to as foraging and harvesting gear. Early humans relied on foraging for food, and foraging has been a feature of human life for thousands of years. Foraging has recently gained popularity again as a way to get fresh, locally grown food and establish a connection with nature. It is crucial to have the proper equipment in order to successfully forage and collect wild foods. The equipment required will depend on the environment being examined and the resources being sought after. Foragers may want to take into consideration using baskets, knives, gloves, and digging tools as crucial pieces of equipment.

Baskets

Foragers need baskets because they provide a safe and effective way to transport foraged items. Indigenous peoples all throughout the world have used them for thousands of years, and they are still commonly utilized today. A variety of materials, including braided grasses and bark and recycled plastic or metal, can be used to create baskets. Depending on the materials being harvested and the forager's tastes, they come in various sizes and shapes. Some baskets are made to be carried by hand, while others are meant to be worn on the back.

Foraging with a basket has a number of benefits, one of which is the convenience of hands-free collection. As a result, the forager can carefully gather objects like berries or nuts with both hands without worrying about where to store them. When foraging in locations with steep terrain or unstable ground, this is very helpful. Additionally, baskets offer a secure manner to carry foraged goods without risking damage. For instance, fragile items like berries or mushrooms that are carried in a bag or pocket risk being crushed or injured. These things can be moved carefully and securely in baskets, preserving their freshness and integrity.

Foraging baskets have the added advantage of frequently being more environmentally friendly than plastic or other synthetic materials. Natural baskets made of willow or grass are biodegradable and less harmful to the environment than plastic bags or containers. Baskets can be both useful and visually beautiful in addition to being utilitarian. The skill and beauty of handmade baskets, which can be works of art in and of themselves, are appreciated by many foragers. Foraging with a handwoven basket can provide a sense of beauty and connection to the outdoors.

Foragers use baskets as versatile and necessary tools. They offer a way to gather things without using your hands, move them gently, and store them in a way that's good for the environment. They can enhance the foraging experience by bringing a sense of beauty and connection and by being aesthetically pleasant.

Knives

Because they make it possible to harvest and prepare wild edibles, knives are an essential piece of equipment for foragers. They come in a wide variety of sizes and shapes, each of which is tailored to the specific needs of the forager as well as the particular responsibilities at hand. One of the primary applications of foraging is using a knife to harvest various plant resources, including fruits, nuts, and other plant parts. A clean cut, which reduces the amount of harm done to the plant and increases the possibility of a bountiful harvest, is produced by a knife that is sharp. In addition, knives can be used to peel bark, slice shoots and stems, and dig up roots.

Not only are knives beneficial for harvesting, but they also help in preparing wild foods for consumption, which is another important purpose for knives. It is possible to scale and gut fish, skin and butcher game, and dice fruits and vegetables. Fish can also be cleaned and gutted. In addition to this, it can be used to assist in the opening of shells such as oysters or clam shells. When it comes to foraging, having a knife that is versatile is another advantage. Because it may be put to a wide variety of uses, a knife of good quality and sharpness is an asset that should be brought along on any excursion that involves foraging. Foragers may carry many knives with them, including one with a wider blade designed for more difficult tasks and another with a smaller, folding blade designed for more detailed work.

When choosing a knife for foraging, it is absolutely necessary to pay attention to both the durability of the blade and the ease with which the user can grip the handle. The blade should be sturdy and able to withstand hard use for an extended period of time, and the handle should be comfortable and easy to hold. Some foragers like the more traditional look of a handle made of wood, while others could choose a handle made of more modern material such as plastic or rubber instead.

Knives are an essential piece of equipment for foragers due to the fact that they enable the collecting and preparation of a wide variety of wild edibles. With the assistance of a razor-sharp, high-quality knife, foragers are able to make accurate cuts, prepare food for consumption, and benefit from the full wealth that the natural world has to offer.

Gloves

Gloves are essential for foragers because they provide comfort and protection when they are scavenging and handling wild foods. They can be made of a wide variety of materials and have a variety of designs, all of which are determined by the task at hand and the preferences of the forager. When out foraging, one of the most important functions that gloves should fulfill is protecting the wearer's hands. Protecting one's hands from dangers such as thorns, prickles, and other natural plants can be accomplished by wearing gloves. As a consequence of this, the risk of injury is decreased, and the forager is able to focus on their work without being troubled or diverted in any way.

Another scenario in which gloves come in handy is when one is handling wild delicacies like nettles, which have stinging hairs that have the potential to harm the skin. Wearing gloves protects foragers against the possibility of experiencing an allergic response or getting stung while handling these plants. Gloves offer a number of benefits, including protection, warmth, and comfort. Foragers may choose to wear gloves made of waterproof or insulated materials when they are out searching for food when the weather is cold or wet. This will help keep their hands warm and dry. Even in difficult conditions, this can make the experience of hunting and gather more enjoyable.

When it comes to the safe handling and collection of wild foods, gloves are an essential piece of equipment for foragers because of the protection, comfort, and versatility they provide. When looking for gloves to use for foraging, it is essential to pay attention to both the construction and the materials used. Foragers have the choice of wearing gloves constructed from a variety of materials, including wool, natural leather, or synthetic materials such as neoprene or nylon. The gloves ought to be comfortable and provide enough dexterity so that the wearer can handle small or delicate objects like berries and mushrooms without difficulty. Foragers can improve the quality of their experience and make it safer by wearing gloves that are designed for the tasks they will be performing.

How to Identify the Plants using Google Lens

Google Lens is an image recognition tool that enables users to recognize items and access data about them using the camera on their smartphone. Despite not being specifically made for foraging, Google Lens can be useful for identifying wild plants and mushrooms.

Foragers can use Google Lens to take a picture of a wild plant or mushroom they come across. Machine learning techniques will be used by the technology to analyze the image and provide details about the species, such as its name, traits, and prospective applications. Foragers who are unsure about the local plant species or who want to confirm the identity of a certain plant or mushroom may find this to be of special use.

Additionally, Google Lens can assist foragers in recognizing dangerous or harmful species, which is crucial for beginning foragers who might not have a thorough understanding of the local flora. But it's important to remember that Google Lens shouldn't be

your only resource for foraging information. Before consuming any wild plant or mushroom, it is crucial to confirm the identity using other sources and professional advice.

Here's how to identify plants while foraging with Google Lens:

Install the Google Lens app first.

Installing Google Lens on your phone is the first step. The app may be downloaded from the App Store or Google Play Store and is compatible with both iOS and Android devices.

The second step, launch Google Lens

Please start the app after installation, then point your camera at the plant you want to identify. The photograph will be automatically scanned by Google Lens, which will then collect details about the plant.

Step 3, take a photo of the plant

Let's say Google Lens is unable to recognize the plant on its own. In such an instance, you can center the plant in the camera viewfinder and take a picture of it by tapping the camera icon on the app.

Step 4, Examine the plant image

Google Lens will examine the image once it has been taken and provide details about the plant. This could include the plant's name, species, traits, and other important details.

Step 5, verify the plant identification

Before ingesting a plant or using it medicinally, it is crucial to confirm its identity. To confirm the plant identification, you can compare the data provided by Google Lens with other sources, such as field guides or professional advice.

Step 6, write down the plant's details

Once the plant has been identified, it is a good idea to write down the details in a notebook or database. Included are the plant's common and scientific names, traits, and any relevant uses or warnings.

Step 7, repeat the process

You can carry out this procedure with more plants you find while foraging. Expanding your understanding of the local flora and learning new plant names can both be accomplished with the help of Google Lens.

In conclusion, foragers who are inexperienced or are unfamiliar with the local plant species may find it useful to use Google Lens to identify plants when foraging. Google Lens should be utilized as an additional tool to improve your foraging experience rather than as the only source of information.

CHAPTER THREE

WHERE TO FORAGE?

*

Finding wild food sources might be difficult because of the expansion of industrial agriculture and urbanization. This chapter will examine the various foraging locations and the kinds of food that can be found there.

Forest: One of the most popular sites for foragers to find food is the forest. There are many different edible plants and mushrooms in the forest. Wild berries including blueberries, raspberries, and blackberries are among the most prevalent plants in the forest. These berries taste great and are rich in vitamins and minerals. The woodland is also home to numerous types of mushrooms, such as morels, chanterelles, and boletes. But it's important to remember that some mushrooms can be deadly, so it's important to know how to identify mushrooms or get advice from a professional before eating.

There are additional wild plants in the forest that are safe to consume besides berries and mushrooms. For instance, you can use cattails, wild garlic, and dandelion greens in salads, soups, and stews. It is crucial to understand how to appropriately identify these plants and make sure they are uncontaminated.

One thing to think about when foraging in the forest is how it will affect the environment. It's crucial to harvest plants and mushrooms in a sustainable manner, taking only what is required while leaving enough for the environment to thrive.

Beach: Although it may not seem like a particularly obvious spot to forage, the beach is a great place to find food. Seafood can be found in abundance at the beach, including clams, mussels, oysters, and crabs. In addition to being delicious, these shellfish are also quite high in protein and low in fat. Seaweed found on beaches is also a great source of antioxidants, vitamins, and minerals. It is crucial to consult with local officials to make sure the region is safe before foraging on the beach. The food may be hazardous in some locations due to pollution or dangerous microorganisms. Additionally, it's important to be knowledgeable about the tides and only gathers shellfish at low tide. Before eating any shellfish, it is crucial to confirm that it is alive and healthy.

Parks and other Green Spaces: You can find plenty of food to forage for in parks and other green spaces. Community gardens and orchards are only two examples of parks that have specific spaces for growing fruits and vegetables. These locations offer a great chance to pick fresh food and are frequently accessible to the general public. Wild plants that are safe to eat, like edible flowers, herbs, and greens, can also be found in parks and other green areas. Sorrel, purslane, and chickweed are a few of the frequently encountered edible plants in parks. However, it is crucial to make sure that these plants weren't exposed to any pesticides or other toxins prior to eating.

When foraging in parks and other open areas, it's important to keep in mind that these areas may be overseen by local government officials, who may have rules and regulations surrounding food collection. It is crucial to consult with local authorities and guarantee that any food harvested is done so sustainably and responsibly before foraging in these areas.

Urban settings: Although it may not seem evident, foraging in urban settings can be a terrific method to find healthy, fresh food. Food-growing spaces, such as community gardens or urban farms, are found in many metropolitan places. These locations offer a great chance to pick fresh food and are frequently accessible to the general public. Fruit trees or other food plants can also grow in public areas like parks, vacant lots, or by the sides of the road. Dandelions, purslane, and wild garlic are a few of the frequently found edible plants in metropolitan environments.

It is crucial to make sure that any food gathered from urban areas has not been polluted with toxins or other dangerous compounds. Foraging, for instance, is not advised near busy roadsides or in places with a lot of industrial activity. Additionally, it's crucial to respect private property and ask permission before harvesting there.

Rural Regions: Farmland and other rural regions make great places to forage for food. Like strawberries or apples, many farms raise crops that are available for picking by the general public. In addition, edible wild plants including blackberries, elderberries, and wild plums can be growing in these locations.

It is crucial to respect the landowners' and farmers' property rights when foraging in rural areas. It is also crucial to make sure that all food collection is done ethically and sustainably. It is not advisable to forage while trampling crops or removing all the fruit from a tree.

CHAPTER FOUR
DO'S AND DON'T'S
*

It can be exciting and enjoyable to go foraging for wild plants, but in order to do it properly and sustainably, it's important to remember some dos and don'ts. The following are some general principles:

Dos:

1. Acquire accurate plant identification skills before you start foraging. Use a trustworthy guidebook or enroll in a foraging class before you begin. Inaccurate identification can result in ingesting poisonous plants, which is dangerous.

2. Pick locations that are far from traffic and other pollution-producing factors. Try to locate regions that haven't seen a lot of human habitation, such as a forest or meadow. These places may have seen harmful chemical absorption by plants, which could be dangerous for your health.

3. Take only what you require, leaving plenty for wildlife and other foragers. By following this procedure, the ecology is preserved and the plant population is maintained. Avoid harming the plant's root system at all costs because doing so could make it challenging for the plant to recover and grow.

4. Refrain from picking invasive plants or endangered species that could harm the ecosystem. Before going out to forage, it's important to complete your homework because some plants can be legally protected. Additionally, some plants have the potential to expand quickly, outcompete native species, and be invasive.

5. Treat the environment and the plants with care. Be careful not to damage the natural environment when you are foraging. Moreover, express gratitude to the plant for its gift and leave an offering, such as some water or your hair. Based on ancient customs, this activity expresses appreciation and respect for the plant and the soil.

6. Please keep a record of what you consume and where it comes from. To keep track of what you've collected, note the plant, the location, and the date of harvest. Additionally, it ensures that you aren't ingesting excessive amounts from one place.

7. Prepare the plants you foraged before eating them. Cooking helps remove dangerous poisons and facilitates the digestion of the plant. Cooking can also improve the flavor of the plant and make it more pleasant.

8. Disseminate your expertise to others. Foraging is a fantastic opportunity to get closer to nature and discover the surroundings. Please educate others about what you've discovered so they can enjoy the advantages of foraging as well.

Don'ts:

1. Never go foraging without being properly identified. Inaccurate identification can result in ingesting poisonous plants, which is dangerous. Know what you're looking for and how to recognize it before you begin.

2. Avoid foraging in regions that have been chemically or pesticide-treated. These substances have the potential to be unhealthy for you and infect the plants you are collecting.

3. Avoid foraging in prohibited or off-limits locations. Foraging in locations that are legally prohibited may result in fines or other legal repercussions.

BOOK 3: IDENTIFYING EDIBLE WILD PLANTS

HOW TO IDENTIFY EDIBLE WILD PLANTS
*

There are a variety of plants, animals, and ecosystems to discover in the natural world, which is a source of curiosity and awe. The ability of plants to support life on earth is one of these wonders. Plants are an integral part of our daily life, serving as food for both humans and animals as well as medicines and cultural icons. Even the most seasoned naturalist may find it difficult to identify wild plants because not all plants are created equal.

Learning to identify and comprehend the numerous plant species that flourish in our environment is the goal of plant identification. Applying this knowledge can be done in a variety of ways, including protecting endangered animals and hunting for wild food. This chapter will examine the significance of correctly identifying wild plants and all of their advantages.

The ability to use wild plants as a food source is among the most persuasive arguments for doing so. Both humans and animals can find good sustenance in wild plants. There are numerous edible wild plants that can be used in a variety of cuisines. Knowing whether wild plants are edible might be useful in survival circumstances where access to conventional food sources may be scarce or nonexistent. In recent years, foraging for wild food has also grown in popularity as more people look to re-establish their connection to nature and lessen their dependency on processed and factory-farmed foods.

Identifying wild plants can also be quite useful in medicine. Some untamed plants have therapeutic qualities that can be utilized to treat a range of illnesses. For people who are interested in natural or alternative medicine or who might not have access to contemporary medical facilities, knowing how to identify these plants might be helpful. Identifying and using wild plants can be a significant way to maintain cultural knowledge and traditions. Wild plants have long been utilized in traditional medicine.

Identification of wild plants can be important for conservation efforts in addition to the advantages it offers to individuals. Knowing a plant's range and population can help conservationists better defend the species against dangers like habitat loss and overharvesting. For conservation efforts to be successful and to ensure the survival of these species for future generations, it can be essential to identify and monitor rare or endangered plant species.

For safety purposes, it may sometimes be required to identify wild plants. Wild plants can sometimes be poisonous or hazardous to both people and animals. By recognizing these plants, people can lessen their risk of damage or disease by avoiding inadvertent ingestion of or contact with dangerous plants. For people who spend time in nature, such as hikers or campers, being able to recognize dangerous plants can be a crucial safety measure.

Finally, recognizing wild plants can be important from a cultural perspective. Numerous untamed plants have cultural value and are employed in rituals and traditional behaviors. In addition to fostering a greater understanding and respect for many cultures, identifying these plants can assist to preserve cultural traditions and knowledge.

It can be thrilling and enjoyable to identify wild plants, but it can also be difficult. It necessitates thorough observation and evaluation of the traits, habitat, and growing stage of the plant. Here, we'll discuss the value of observation and evaluation in recognizing wild plants and offer some advice on how to carry out these processes successfully.

Observation

To identify a wild plant, one must first observe its characteristics. To do this, look at the plant's leaves, stem, blossoms, and other distinctive characteristics. You can exclude certain possibilities and determine the plant's family or genus by closely evaluating the plant's physical traits. Here are some pointers for identifying a wild plant's traits:

Start with the leaves: A plant's leaves can reveal important details about its identity. Look at the leaves' arrangement, size, and form. Are they in opposition or rotation? Is their structure simple or complex? Are they hairy or hairless? Any distinguishing characteristics, such as serrated edges or peculiar patterns, should be noted.

Look at the stem: Important hints can also be found in a plant's stem. Look at the stem's color, texture, and shape. Is it herbaceous or woody? Is it square or round? Are there any recognizable patterns or marks on the stem?

A look at the flowers The most distinguishing characteristic of a plant is frequently its flowers. Look at the blooms' size, shape, and color. Do they live alone or in groups? Are there flowers or sepals on them? Do the blooms have any recognizable patterns or markings?

Other characteristics to look for include: There might be additional characteristics that can assist in identifying a wild plant in addition to the leaves, stem, and flowers. For instance, while some plants have thorns or spines, others have distinctive fruits or seed pods.

Assessment

The following step is to evaluate the plant's habitat, growth stage, and health after seeing its physical traits. This can help clarify the identity of the plant and provide essential information about its ecological niche. Here are some guidelines for determining the habitat, stage of growth, and health of a wild plant:

Think about the plant's environment: A plant's habitat might offer crucial hints about its identification. Note the plant's growing conditions, including the soil, sunlight exposure, and moisture content. Is it in a swamp, meadow, or forest? Does it like soil that is acidic or alkaline? Does it need constant hydration or is it tolerant to drought?

Examine the stage of growth of the plant: A plant's stage of development can also be used to identify it. Keep an eye out for the plant's size, form, and any reproductive components like flowers or fruit. Is it an established plant or a new seedling? Is it in full bloom or has fruit already appeared?

Analyze the health of the plant: A plant's health might offer hints as to its identity and be crucial in assessing its possible applications. Generally speaking, a healthy plant has glossy leaves, a strong stem, and rapid development. Search for indications of disease, insect damage, and additional stressors like nutrient deficiency or drought.

Identification of wild plants requires observation and evaluation. You can eliminate the options and determine the family or genus of the plant by closely examining its physical traits and evaluating its habitat, growth stage, and health. Although it might be difficult to identify wild plants, it can also be a gratifying experience that deepens your understanding of the natural world. You can become an expert at identifying wild plants and learn more about the biological systems that surround us with time and effort.

When recognizing wild plants, a few crucial traits might assist separate one species from another. These traits include the color, texture, and shape of the stem; the shape, color, and arrangement of the flowers; and the structure of the fruit or seed. People can exclude certain possibilities and determine the family or genus of the plant by paying great attention to these characteristics.

Some of a plant's most distinguishing features are frequently the shape, arrangement, and feel of its leaves. Simple or compound leaves, lobed or unlobed, toothed or smooth, and placed in a variety of patterns on the stem are all possible. People may frequently identify a plant's family or genus by looking at its leaf features.

Similarly to this, stem color, shape, and texture can offer vital hints for identifying plants. While some plants have flexible and delicate herbaceous stems, others have woody stems. The stem might be smooth and green or rough and brown, with a wide range in both color and texture.

A plant's flower's shape, color, and arrangement are frequently its most recognized features. Flowers come in a variety of colors, from vivid reds and yellows to subdued blues and purples, and can be found growing alone or in groups. Given that some flowers have funnel-, bell-, or star-shaped shapes, the form of the flower can also be a useful distinguishing characteristic.

Last but not least, a plant's fruit or seed structure might offer crucial hints for identification. While some plants produce fruit that is dry and hard, others produce fruit that is soft and delicious. The size and shape of the fruit or seed can be significant as well; some seeds include wings or barbs to aid in spreading.

It is significant to remember that, depending on age, growth conditions, and genetic variation, these distinguishing traits can differ significantly within the same plant species. As a result, it is crucial to take into account a variety of traits while identifying a plant and to seek confirmation from a variety of sources.

Numerous more elements can aid in the identification of wild plants in addition to these major identifying traits. The habitat, growth patterns, and aroma of the plant are some of these. While some plants like certain types of soil, others prefer moist or dry environments. The way a plant grows can also be revealing; some plants grow tall and upright, while others spread out and grow low. Last but not least, a plant's scent can be a helpful distinguishing characteristic. Some plants have distinct aromas that can help eliminate some of the possibilities.

To sum up, important distinguishing traits such as leaf shape, arrangement, and texture; stem color, shape, and texture; flower shape, color, and arrangement; and fruit or seed structure are essential for identifying wild plants. People can exclude certain possibilities and determine the family or genus of the plant by paying great attention to these characteristics. Wild plant identification can also be aided by aspects including environment, growth patterns, and aroma. Anyone may become an expert at identifying wild plants and have a deeper grasp of the natural world around them with time and effort.

CHAPTER TWO

UNIVERSAL EDIBILITY TEST
*

As has been underlined, it is crucial to discern between edible plants that are safe to eat and those that are poisonous or otherwise unfit for consumption when foraging for wild plants. The Universal Edibility Test, a set of procedures intended to assess whether a plant is safe to eat, is one method of evaluating the edibility of a wild plant. The procedures for carrying out the Universal Edibility Test will be described in this chapter. What is the Universal Edibility Test, first of all? The Universal Edibility Test is a method that can be used to assess if a wild plant is suitable for consumption. Foragers, hikers, and other outdoor enthusiasts who might come upon wild plants while enjoying nature will find it to be a useful tool. Identification of the plant is the first step in the test, which also includes testing for allergies and contact toxicity as well as internal toxicity.

Choose the Plant: Correct identification of the plant is the first stage in determining whether a wild plant is edible. An expert's advice or employing a field guide can both be used to accomplish this. It is significant to remember that although many plants resemble one another, even closely related species can exhibit widely differing levels of toxicity. Consequently, confirm the identity of the plant before doing the test.

Checking for allergies: An allergy test must be performed before ingesting any plant material. You can check for irritation or redness by rubbing a little piece of the plant on your skin, waiting a few hours, and then checking again. The following move can be made if there is no reaction.

Test for Contact Toxicity: The next step is to conduct a contact toxicity test to determine whether the plant has the ability to damage someone when it comes into touch with their skin. To achieve this, press a little piece of the plant against the skin for a few hours while keeping an eye out for any discomfort or redness. The following move can be made if there is no reaction.

Internal Toxicity Test: Testing for internal toxicity, or the likelihood that the plant may hurt someone when consumed, is the most important phase in the Universal Edibility Test. This can be accomplished by preparing a little quantity of the plant and eating it in a regulated environment. How to carry out this test is described in the stages below:

How to detect bitterness: Take a little bit of the plant and taste it. Do not continue with the test if the plant is extremely bitter or gives off a burning feeling.

Make a little preparation of the plant: Pick a modest amount, like a quarter of a cup, then prepare it just like you would food. To make the plant suitable for ingestion, this may need boiling, roasting, or other forms of preparation.

After ingesting the plant, wait at least eight hours before checking for any signs of disease, such as nausea, vomiting, or diarrhoea. The herb can be consumed safely if no symptoms appear.

It is crucial to remember that even if a plant passes the Universal Edibility Test, it should still be consumed cautiously and in moderation. Consuming high amounts of any plant can result in stomach distress, and some plants may have long-term impacts on the body that are not immediately apparent.

In conclusion, the Universal Edibility Test is a useful tool for determining if wild plants are edible. By using the methods described above, people may decide whether a plant is safe to consume and prevent any negative impacts that may result from ingesting hazardous plants. However, even plants that have passed the Universal Edibility Test should always be used with caution and in moderation. Anyone can become an expert at identifying and evaluating the edibility of wild plants with enough time and effort, and they'll also learn more about the natural world around them.

CHAPTER THREE
TOP 60 EDIBLE WILD PLANTS
*

Humans have always been able to survive by eating vegetation. We have always been enthralled by the astounding variety of plants because they give us vital nutrients and a dizzying number of flavors and gastronomic pleasures. This chapter will examine the top 60 edible plants, each of which is delectable and has special nutritional advantages. These plants will be separated into the following categories: bark, seaweed, nettle family, knotweed, shoots and stems, leaves, nuts, seeds, and grains.

HERBS, TREES, AND SHRUBS

Cinnamon

A spice made from the bark of several species of trees in the genus Cinnamomum.

Where to find it	Native to Sri Lanka and southern India, but now grown in many parts of the world.
Edible parts	The tree's inner bark is dried and ground into a powder used to flavor sweet and savory dishes.
Flavor	Sweet, warm, and slightly spicy.
Caution	Cinnamon can cause allergic reactions in some people.
Uses	Often used to flavor baked goods, drinks, and savory dishes. Also used in traditional medicine to help lower blood sugar and cholesterol levels.
Nutritional value	Cinnamon is a good source of antioxidants and contains small amounts of vitamins and minerals.

Lavender

A fragrant, flowering plant with purple or blue flowers and green leaves.

Where to find it	Native to the Mediterranean, but now grown in many parts of the world.
Edible parts	The flowers can be used in cooking as a garnish or flavoring.
Flavor	Floral, slightly sweet, and slightly bitter.
Caution	Lavender oil can be toxic if ingested in large quantities.
Uses	Often used in aromatherapy and skin care products for its calming properties. It can also be used to flavor desserts and drinks.
Nutritional value	Lavender is not a significant source of vitamins or antioxidants.

Lemon

A small evergreen tree with fragrant, yellow fruit.

Where to find it	Native to Asia, but now grown in many parts of the world.
Edible parts	The fruit can be used in cooking, usually as a flavoring for sweet and savory dishes.
Flavor	Sour, acidic, and slightly sweet.
Caution	None.
Uses	Often used to flavor desserts, drinks, and savory dishes. It can also be used in cleaning and disinfecting products for its antibacterial properties.
Nutritional value	Lemons are a good vitamin C source and contain small amounts of other vitamins and minerals.

Peppermint

A perennial herb with green leaves and purple flowers, often used for its minty flavor.

Where to find it	Native to Europe and Asia, but now grown in many parts of the world.
Edible parts	The leaves can be used fresh or dried to flavor teas, desserts, and savory dishes.
Flavor	Cool, minty, and slightly sweet.
Caution	Peppermint can cause heartburn and digestive issues in some people.
Uses	Often used to relieve symptoms of colds, headaches, and digestive issues. It can also be used to flavor desserts, drinks, and sauces.
Nutritional value	Peppermint is a good source of vitamins A and C and small amounts of other vitamins and minerals.

Sage

A woody, perennial herb with grey-green leaves and purple flowers.

Where to find it	Native to the Mediterranean, but now grown in many parts of the world.
Edible parts	The leaves can be used in cooking, usually as a flavoring for meat dishes.
Flavor	Earthy, slightly bitter, and slightly peppery.
Caution	None.
Uses	Often used in traditional medicine for its antibacterial and anti-inflammatory properties. It can also be used to flavor stuffing and sausage.
Nutritional value	Sage is a good vitamin K source and contains small amounts of other vitamins and minerals.

Thym

A perennial herb with small, green leaves and purple or pink flowers.

Where to find it	Native to the Mediterranean, but now grown in many parts of the world.
Edible parts	The leaves can be used in cooking as a flavoring for meat dishes and sauces.
Flavor	Earthy, slightly minty, and slightly sweet.
Caution	None.
Uses	Often used in traditional medicine for its antiseptic and expectorant properties. It can also be used to flavor soups, stews, and marinades.
Nutritional value	Thyme is a good vitamin C source and contains small amounts of other vitamins and minerals. It is also high in antioxidants.

SHOOTS AND STEMS

Asparagus

A perennial flowering plant with tall, feathery foliage and edible shoots.

Where to find it	Native to Europe, but now grown in many parts of the world.
Edible parts	The young shoots can be eaten raw or cooked.
	Flavor: Earthy, slightly sweet, and slightly bitter.
Caution	Asparagus can cause allergic reactions in some people.
Uses	Often used in cooking as a side dish or in salads. It can also be used in traditional medicine as a diuretic and to treat various ailments.
Nutritional value	Asparagus is a good source of vitamins A, C, and K, folate, and other minerals.

Bamboo

A group of perennial evergreen plants with woody stems and edible shoots.

Where to find it	Native to Asia, but now grown in many parts of the world.
Edible parts	The young shoots can be eaten raw or cooked.
Flavor	Mild, slightly sweet, and slightly nutty.
Caution	Some varieties of bamboo shoots can be toxic if not prepared correctly.
Uses	Often used in Asian cooking in stir-fries, soups, and salads. It can also be used in traditional medicine to treat various ailments.
Nutritional value	Bamboo shoots are a good source of vitamins A, C, and E, as well as dietary fiber and other minerals.

Bean

A legume plant with edible pods and shoots.

Where to find it	Native to Central and South America, but now grown in many parts of the world.
Edible parts	The young shoots and leaves can be eaten raw or cooked.
Flavor	Earthy, slightly sweet, and slightly bitter.
Caution	Some varieties of bean shoots can be toxic if not prepared correctly.
Uses	Often used in cooking salads, soups, and stir-fries. It can also be used in traditional medicine to treat various ailments.
Nutritional value	Bean shoots are a good source of vitamins A, C, and K, dietary fiber, and other minerals.

Broccoli

A cruciferous vegetable with green flowering heads and edible stems.

Where to find it	Native to the Mediterranean, but now grown in many parts of the world.
Edible parts	The stems and florets can be eaten raw or cooked.
Flavor	Earthy, slightly sweet, and slightly bitter.
Caution	Broccoli can cause digestive issues in some people.
Uses	Often used in cooking salads, stir-fries, and soups. It can also be used in traditional medicine to treat various ailments.
Nutritional value	Broccoli is a good source of vitamins A, C, and K, dietary fiber, and other minerals. It is also high in antioxidants.

Brussels Sprouts

A cruciferous vegetable with small, green heads and edible stems.

Where to find it	Native to Europe, but now grown in many parts of the world.
Edible parts	The stems and sprouts can be eaten raw or cooked.
Flavor	Earthy, slightly sweet, and slightly bitter.
	Caution: Brussels sprouts can cause digestive issues in some people.
Uses	Often used in cooking as a side dish or in salads. It can also be used in traditional medicine to treat various ailments.
Nutritional value	Brussels sprouts are a good source of vitamins A, C, and K, dietary fiber, and other minerals. They are also high in antioxidants.

Pea

A legume plant with edible pods and shoots.

Where to find it	Native to Asia, but now grown in many parts of the world.
Edible parts	The young shoots and leaves can be eaten raw or cooked.
Flavor	Sweet, slightly grassy, and slightly nutty.
Caution	Some varieties of pea shoots can be toxic if not prepared correctly.
Uses	Often used in cooking salads, stir-fries, and soups. It can also be used in traditional medicine to treat various ailments.
Nutritional value	Pea shoots are a good source of vitamins A, C, and K, dietary fiber, and other minerals. They are also high in antioxidants and protein.

LEAVES

Basil

An herbaceous plant with fragrant, green leaves.

Where to find it	Originally from tropical regions of central Africa and Southeast Asia, but now grown in many parts of the world.
Edible parts	The leaves can be eaten raw or cooked.
Flavor	Sweet, peppery, and slightly minty.
Caution	None.
Uses	Often used in cooking salads, soups, pesto, and as a garnish. It can also be used in traditional medicine to treat various ailments.
Nutritional value	Basil leaves are a good source of vitamins A and K and other minerals and antioxidants.

Dandelion

A typical weed with serrated, dark green leaves.

Where to find it	Found all over the world, in temperate regions.
Edible parts	The leaves can be eaten raw or cooked.
Flavor	Slightly bitter.
Caution	It can cause allergic reactions in some people.
Uses	Often used in salads and teas. It can also be used in traditional medicine to treat various ailments.
Nutritional value	Dandelion leaves are a good source of vitamins A and C and other minerals and antioxidants.

Kale

A leafy vegetable with green or purple leaves.

Where to find it	Originally from the eastern Mediterranean and Asia Minor, but now grown in many parts of the world.
Edible parts	The leaves can be eaten raw or cooked.
Flavor	Slightly bitter and earthy.
	Caution: None.
Uses	Often used in salads, smoothies, and soups. It can also be used in traditional medicine to treat various ailments.
Nutritional value	Kale leaves are a good source of vitamins A, C, and K and other minerals and antioxidants.

34

Lettuce

A leafy vegetable with light green leaves.

Where to find it	Originated in the Mediterranean and the Middle East but has now grown in many parts of the world.
Edible parts	The leaves can be eaten raw or cooked.
Flavor	Mild and slightly sweet.
	Caution: None.
Uses	Often used in salads and sandwiches. It can also be used in traditional medicine to treat various ailments.
Nutritional value	Lettuce leaves are a good source of vitamins A and C and other minerals and antioxidants.

Spinach

A leafy vegetable with dark green leaves.

Where to find it	Native to central and southwestern Asia, but now grown in many parts of the world.
Edible parts	The leaves can be eaten raw or cooked.
Flavor	Mild and slightly sweet.
Caution	It should not be eaten in significant quantities by people with certain health conditions, such as kidney stones.
Uses	Often used in salads, smoothies, and as a cooked vegetable. It can also be used in traditional medicine to treat various ailments.
Nutritional value	Spinach leaves are a good source of vitamins A, C, and K and other minerals and antioxidants.

Watercress

Short description: A semi-aquatic plant with small, round leaves.

Where to find it	Native to Europe and Asia, but now grown in many parts of the world.
Edible parts	The leaves can be eaten raw or cooked.
Flavor	Peppery and slightly bitter.
Caution	It should not be eaten in significant quantities by people with certain health conditions, such as thyroid problems.
Uses	Often used in salads and sandwiches. It can also be used in traditional medicine to treat various ailments, including coughs, colds, and skin conditions.
Nutritional value	Watercress leaves are a good source of vitamins A, C, and K and other minerals and antioxidants.

NUTS

Almonds

Almonds are tree nuts with a hard outer shell and an edible kernel.

Where to find it	Almonds are grown in many parts of the world, including California, Spain, and Australia.
Edible parts	The kernel or meat of the almond is edible.
Flavor	Almonds have a mild, nutty flavor.
Caution	Some people may have an allergy to almonds.
Use	Almonds are often used as a snack, as well as in baked goods, desserts, and as a topping for salads and other dishes
Nutritional value	Almonds are high in healthy fats, protein, fiber, vitamin E, magnesium, and other nutrients.

Brazil nuts

Brazil nuts are large, round nuts that grow on trees in the Amazon rainforest.

Where to find it	Brazil nuts are primarily grown in Brazil, Bolivia, and Peru.
Edible parts	The kernel or meat of the Brazil nut is edible.
Flavor	Brazil nuts have a rich, creamy flavor.
Caution	Brazil nuts are high in selenium, which can be toxic in large amounts.
Use	Brazil nuts are often eaten as a snack or used in baking and other recipes.
Nutritional value	Brazil nuts are high in healthy fats, protein, fiber, and other nutrients, including selenium.

Cashews

Cashews are a type of tree nut with a kidney-shaped kernel.

Where to find it	Cashews are primarily grown in Brazil, India, and Vietnam.
Edible parts	The kernel or meat of the cashew is edible.
Flavor	Cashews have a mild, buttery flavor.
Caution	Some people may have an allergy to cashews.
Use	Cashews are often used in cooking, as well as in snacks, candy, and desserts.
Nutritional value	Cashews are high in healthy fats, protein, and other nutrients, including magnesium and zinc.

Hazelnuts

Hazelnuts are tree nuts with a hard outer shell and an edible kernel.

Where to find it	Hazelnuts are grown in many parts of the world, including Turkey, Italy, and the United States.
Edible parts	The kernel or meat of the hazelnut is edible.
Flavor	Hazelnuts have a rich, nutty flavor.
Caution	Some people may have an allergy to hazelnuts.
Use	Hazelnuts are often used in baking and spread like Nutella and chocolate.
Nutritional value	Hazelnuts are high in healthy fats, protein, and other nutrients, including vitamin E, magnesium, and fiber.

Pistachio

Pistachios are small, greenish nuts with a hard, beige-colored shell and a greenish-yellow interior. They have a slightly sweet and nutty flavor.

Where to find it	Pistachios are primarily grown in the Middle East but are also cultivated in the United States and other parts of the world.
Edible parts	The pistachio kernel inside the shell is edible.
Flavor	Slightly sweet and nutty.
Caution	Pistachios may cause allergic reactions in some people.
Use	Pistachios are a good source of protein, fiber, and healthy fats. They can be eaten as a snack, used in baking and cooking, or made into pistachio butter.
Nutritional value	Pistachios are a good source of protein, fiber, and healthy fats. They also contain vitamins and minerals, such as vitamin B6, thiamine, copper, and phosphorus. Additionally, pistachios are rich in antioxidants, which may help protect against chronic diseases such as heart disease and cancer.

Pecans

Pecans are tree nuts with a hard outer shell and an edible kernel.

Where to find it	Pecans are primarily grown in the southern United States and Mexico.
Edible parts	The kernel or meat of the pecan is edible.
Flavor	Pecans have a rich, buttery flavor.
Caution	Some people may have an allergy to pecans.
Use	Pecans are often used in baking, as well as in snacks.
Nutritional value	Pecans are a good source of healthy fats, fiber, and protein. They also contain vitamins and minerals, such as vitamin E, thiamine, and zinc. Additionally, pecans are rich in antioxidants, which may help protect against chronic diseases such as heart disease and cancer.

SEEDS AND GRAINS

Chia Seeds

Chia seeds are tiny, oval-shaped seeds native to Mexico and Guatemala. They have a mild, nutty flavor.

Where to find it	Chia seeds are grown in many parts of the world, including South America, Australia, and the United States.
Edible parts	The whole chia seed is edible.
Flavor	Mild and nutty.
Caution	Chia seeds may cause allergic reactions in some people.
Use	Chia seeds are a good source of fiber, healthy fats, and antioxidants. They can be added to smoothies and oatmeal or used as a topping for yogurt or salads.
Nutritional value	High in fiber, omega-3 fatty acids, calcium, and antioxidants.

Flaxseed

Flaxseeds are tiny, oval-shaped seeds that are native to the Mediterranean region. They have a slightly nutty flavor.

Where to find it	Flaxseeds are grown in many parts of the world, including Canada, Russia, and the United States.
Edible parts	The whole flaxseed is edible.
Flavor	Slightly nutty.
Caution	Flaxseeds may cause digestive issues if consumed in large quantities.
Use	Flaxseeds are a good source of fiber, healthy fats, and antioxidants. They can be added to baked goods, smoothies, or topping for yogurt or oatmeal.
Nutritional Value	High in fiber, omega-3 fatty acids, lignans, and antioxidants.

Hemp Seeds

Hemp seeds are tiny, oval-shaped seeds that come from the hemp plant. They have a mild, nutty flavor.

Where to find it	Hemp seeds are grown in many parts of the world, including Canada, China, and the United States.
Edible parts	The whole hemp seed is edible.
Flavor	Mild and nutty.
Caution	Hemp seeds may cause allergic reactions in some people.
Use	Hemp seeds are a good source of protein, healthy fats, and antioxidants. They can be added to smoothies and salad or used as a topping for yogurt or oatmeal.
Nutritional value	High in protein, omega-3 fatty acids, magnesium, and antioxidants.

Quinoa

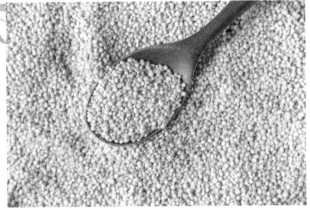

Quinoa is a grain-li native to the Andes region of South America. It has a nutty flavor and a crunchy texture.

Where to find it	Quinoa is grown in many parts of the world, including Peru, Bolivia, and the United States.
Edible parts	The whole quinoa seed is edible.
Flavor	Nutty.
Caution	Quinoa may cause digestive issues in some people.
Use	Quinoa is a good source of protein, fiber, vitamins, and minerals such as magnesium, potassium, and iron. It can be used as a substitute for rice or pasta or added to salads or soups.
Nutritional value	High in protein, fiber, iron, and magnesium.

Sunflower Seeds

Sunflower seeds are tiny, oval-shaped seeds that come from the sunflower plant. They have a slightly nutty flavor and a crunchy texture.

Where to find it	Sunflower seeds are grown in many parts of the world, including Russia, Ukraine, and the United States.
Edible parts	The whole sunflower seed is edible.
Flavor	Slightly nutty.
Caution	Sunflower seeds may cause allergic reactions in some people.
Use	Sunflower seeds are a good source of protein, healthy fats, and vitamins and minerals such as E, magnesium, and selenium. They can be eaten as a snack.
Nutritional value	High in vitamin E, magnesium, selenium, and antioxidants.

BERRIES AND FRUITS

Blackberries

Blackberries are small, dark purple fruits that grow on thorny bushes.

Where can you find it	They grow in temperate climates and are widely cultivated throughout the world.
Edible parts	The entire fruit is edible, including the seeds.
Flavor	They have a sweet and tart flavor and are often used in jams, pies, and desserts.
Caution	They can be difficult to pick due to the thorns on the plant.
Use	Blackberries are a good source of fiber and vitamin C and can improve digestion and boost the immune system.
Nutritional value	They are high in antioxidants, vitamin K, and manganese.

Blueberries

Blueberries are small, round fruits with a blue-purple color.

Where can you find it	They grow in cold climates and are native to North America.
Edible parts	The entire fruit is edible, including the skin and seeds.
Flavor	They have a sweet and slightly tart flavor and are often used in smoothies, baked goods, and salads.
Caution	None known.
Use	Blueberries are a good source of antioxidants and vitamin C and can help improve brain function and prevent chronic diseases.
Nutritional value	They are high in fiber, vitamin C, and vitamin K.

Cranberries

Cranberries are small, tart fruits that grow on low-lying vines.

Where can you find it	They are native to North America and grow in acidic soil.
Edible parts	The entire fruit is edible but is often used in sauces, juices, and baked goods.
Flavor	They have a tart and slightly bitter flavor.
Caution	None known.
Use	Cranberries are a good source of vitamin C and can help prevent urinary tract infections.
Nutritional value	They are high in antioxidants and vitamin C.

Raspberries

Raspberries are small, red berries that grow on thorny bushes.

Where can you find it	They grow in temperate climates and are widely cultivated throughout the world.
Edible parts	The entire fruit is edible, including the seeds.
Flavor	They have a sweet and slightly tart flavor and are often used in jams, pies, and desserts.
Caution	They can be difficult to pick due to the thorns on the plant.
Use	Raspberries are a good fiber and vitamin C source and can improve digestion and boost the immune system.
Nutritional value	They are high in antioxidants, vitamin C, and manganese.

Strawberries

Strawberries are small, red fruits that grow on low-lying plants.

Where can you find it	They are native to Europe but are widely cultivated throughout the world.
Edible parts	The entire fruit is edible but is often used in desserts, jams, and smoothies.
Flavor	They have a sweet and slightly tart flavor.
Caution	None known.
Use	Strawberries are a good source of vitamin C and can help improve heart health.
Nutritional value	They are high in antioxidants, vitamin C, and fiber.

Oranges

Oranges are round fruits with thick, orange skin.

Where can you find it	They are widely cultivated throughout the world.
Edible parts	The fruit's flesh is edible, but the seeds should be avoided.
Flavor	They have a sweet and tangy flavor and are often eaten as a snack or used in juices and desserts.
Caution	None known.
Use	Oranges are a good source of vitamin C and can help boost the immune system and improve skin health.
Nutritional value	They are high in vitamin C and fiber.

BARK

Cinnamon bark

Cinnamon bark comes from the bark of the cinnamon tree and is often used as a spice in cooking or for medicinal purposes.

Where can you find it	Cinnamon trees are native to Sri Lanka but are also grown in other tropical regions such as India, Indonesia, and Brazil.
Edible parts	The bark can be ground into a powder and used as a spice in cooking.
Flavor	Cinnamon has a sweet and spicy flavor.
Caution	Cinnamon contains coumarin, which can be toxic in large doses.
Use	Cinnamon is often used for its anti-inflammatory properties and to help lower blood sugar levels.
Nutritional value	Cinnamon is high in antioxidants.

Dogwood bark

Dogwood bark comes from the bark of the dogwood tree and has been used for medicinal purposes for centuries.

Where can you find it	Dogwood trees are native to North America but can also be found in Asia and Europe.
Edible parts	The bark can be used to make tea.
Flavor	Dogwood bark has a bitter flavor.
Caution	Dogwood bark should be used cautiously as it can cause nausea and vomiting in some people.
Use	Dogwood bark has been used to treat fevers, malaria, and pain.
Nutritional value	Dogwood bark is high in antioxidants.

Oak bark

Oak bark comes from the bark of oak trees and has been used for medicinal purposes for centuries.

Where can you find it	Oak trees are native to the Northern Hemisphere and can be found in North America, Europe, and Asia.
Edible parts	The bark can be used to make tea.
Flavor	Oak bark has a bitter flavor.
Caution	Oak bark should be used cautiously as it can cause nausea and vomiting in some people.
Use	Oak bark has been used to treat diarrhea, fever, and coughs.
Nutritional value	Oak bark is high in antioxidants

.

Pine bark

Pine bark comes from the bark of pine trees and has been used for medicinal purposes for centuries.

Where can you find it	Pine trees are native to the Northern Hemisphere and can be found in North America, Europe, and Asia.Edible parts: The bark can be used to make tea.
Flavor	Pine bark has a bitter flavor.
Caution	Pine bark should be used cautiously as it can cause nausea and vomiting in some people.
Use	Pine bark has been used to treat arthritis, allergies, and skin disorders.
Nutritional value	Pine bark is high in antioxidants.

Slippery elm bark

Slippery elm bark comes from the bark of the slippery elm tree and has been used for medicinal purposes for centuries.

Where can you find it	Slippery elm trees are native to North America.
Edible parts	The bark can make tea or as a thickening agent for soups and stews.
Flavor	Slippery elm bark has a slightly sweet flavor.
Caution	None.
Use	Slippery elm bark has been used to treat sore throats, coughs, and digestive issues.
Nutritional value	Slippery elm bark is high in antioxidants

Willow bark

Willow bark comes from the bark of the willow tree and has been used for medicinal purposes for centuries, particularly for its pain-relieving properties.

Where can you find it	Willow trees are native to the Northern Hemisphere and can be found in North America, Europe, and Asia.
Edible parts	The bark can be used to make tea or tincture.
Flavor	Willow bark has a bitter flavor.
Caution	Willow bark should be used cautiously as it can cause stomach upset, allergic reactions, and interact with certain medications.
Use	Willow bark has been used to treat pain, fever, and inflammation.
Nutritional value	Willow bark is high in salicin, a compound similar to aspirin

SEAWEED

Dulse

Dulse is a red seaweed that grows in the North Atlantic and is commonly used in European and Asian cuisine.

Where can you find it	Dulse is found along the coasts of Canada, Ireland, and Iceland.
Edible parts	The fronds of the seaweed are edible and can be eaten raw or dried and used as a seasoning.
Flavor	Dulse has a salty, smoky flavor.
Caution	Dulse can be high in sodium, so it should be consumed in moderation.
Use	Dulse is often used in soups, salads and as a seasoning for seafood dishes.
Nutritional value	Dulse is high in protein, fiber, and vitamins A and C

.

Hijiki

Hijiki is a brown seaweed that is commonly used in Japanese cuisine.

Where can you find it	Hijiki is found along the coasts of Japan, Korea, and China.
Edible parts	The fronds of the seaweed are edible and are often rehydrated before cooking.
Flavor	Hijiki has a robust and earthy flavor.
Caution	Hijiki can be high in arsenic, so it should be consumed in moderation.
Use	Hijiki is often used in salads, stews, and as a side dish.
Nutritional value	Hijiki is high in fiber, iron, and calcium.

Kelp

Kelp is a brown seaweed that grows in shallow ocean waters and is commonly used in Asian cuisine.

Where can you find it	Kelp is found along the coasts of Japan, Korea, and China.
Edible parts	The seaweed fronds are edible and often used in soups, salads, and as a side dish.
Flavor	Kelp has a slightly sweet, oceanic flavor.
Caution	Kelp can be high in iodine, so it should be consumed in moderation.
Use	Kelp is often used in soups, salads and as a seasoning for seafood dishes.
Nutritional value	Kelp is high in iodine, potassium, and vitamins A and K.

Nori

Nori is a red seaweed commonly used in Japanese cuisine, particularly for making sushi.

Where can you find it	Nori is found along the coasts of Japan and other Pacific Rim countries.
Edible parts	The seaweed fronds are edible and often roasted before being used in cooking.
Flavor	Nori has a nutty, slightly sweet flavor.
Caution	Nori can be high in sodium, so it should be consumed in moderation.
Use	Nori is often used to wrap sushi rolls and as a seasoning for rice dishes.
Nutritional value	Nori is high in protein, fiber, and vitamins A and B12.

Sea lettuce

Sea lettuce is a green seaweed that grows in shallow ocean waters and is commonly used in European and Asian cuisine.

Where can you find it	Sea lettuce is found along the coasts of Europe, Asia, and North America.
Edible parts	The fronds of the seaweed are edible and can be eaten raw or cooked.
Flavor	Sea lettuce has a mild, slightly sweet flavor.
Caution	None.
Use	Sea lettuce is often used in salads, soups, and as a garnish for seafood dishes.
Nutritional value	Sea lettuce is high in protein, fiber, and vitamins A and C.

Wakame

Wakame is a brown seaweed that is commonly used in Japanese cuisine.

Where can you find it	Wakame is found along the coasts of Japan and Korea.
Edible parts	The fronds of the seaweed are edible and are often rehydrated before cooking.
Flavor	Wakame has a sweet, slightly salty flavor.
Caution	Wakame can be high in sodium, so it should be consumed in moderation.
Use	Wakame is often used in soups, salads, and as a side dish.
Nutritional value	Wakame is high in calcium, iron, and vitamins A and C.

NETTLE FAMILY

Dead nettle

Dead nettle is a herbaceous flowering plant with soft, hairy leaves.

Where can you find it	Dead nettle is found throughout Europe and Asia.
Edible parts	The leaves and flowers of dead nettle are edible.
Flavor	Dead nettle has a mild, slightly sweet flavor.
Caution	None known.
Use	Dead nettle can be used in salads or as a cooked vegetable.
Nutritional value	Dead nettle is a good source of vitamins A and C.

Hemp nettle

Img credit: Wild flower finder

Hemp nettle is an annual plant with white or pink flowers.

Where can you find it	Hemp nettle is found throughout Europe and Asia.
Edible parts	The leaves and young shoots of hemp nettle are edible.
Flavor	Hemp nettle has a mild, slightly bitter flavor.
Caution	None known.
Use	Hemp nettle can be used in salads or as a cooked vegetable.
Nutritional value	Hemp nettle is a good source of vitamins A and C.

Stinging nettle

Stinging nettle is a herbaceous perennial plant with stinging hairs on its leaves and stems.

Where can you find it	Stinging nettle is found throughout Europe, Asia, and North America.
Edible parts	The leaves and young shoots of stinging nettle are edible once cooked.
Flavor	Stinging nettle has a nutty, spinach-like flavor.
Caution	Stinging nettle should be handled with gloves to avoid stings.
Use	Stinging nettle can be used in soups, stews, and teas.
Nutritional value	Stinging nettle is a good source of vitamins A and C, iron, and calcium

White dead nettle

White dead nettle is a herbaceous perennial plant with hairy leaves and white flowers.

Where can you find it	White dead nettle is found throughout Europe and Asia.
Edible parts	The leaves and flowers of white dead nettle are edible.
Flavor	White dead nettle has a mild, slightly sweet flavor.
Caution	None known.
Use	White dead nettle can be used in salads or as a cooked vegetable.
Nutritional value	White dead nettle is a good source of vitamins A and C.

Wood nettle

Wood nettle is a herbaceous perennial plant with stinging hairs on its leaves and stems.

Where can you find it	Wood nettle is found throughout North America.
Edible parts	The leaves and young shoots of wood nettle are edible once cooked.
Flavor	Wood nettle has a nutty, spinach-like flavor.
Caution	Wood nettle should be handled with gloves to avoid stings.
Use	Wood nettle can be used in soups, stews, and teas.
Nutritional value	Wood nettle is a good source of vitamins A and C, iron, and calcium.

Yellow dead nettle

Yellow dead nettle is a herbaceous perennial plant with hairy leaves and yellow flowers.

Where can you find it	Yellow dead nettle is found throughout Europe and Asia.
Edible parts	The leaves and flowers of yellow dead nettle are edible.
Flavor	Yellow dead nettle has a mild, slightly sweet flavor.
Caution	None known.
Use	Yellow dead nettle can be used in salads or as garnishes in some meals.
Nutritional Value	Yellow dead nettle is a good source of vitamins A and C and minerals such as calcium and iron. It also contains flavonoids, antioxidants that may have anti-inflammatory and immune-boosting properties. Additionally, yellow dead nettle has been traditionally used to alleviate symptoms of allergies

And respiratory conditions due to its potential antihistamine and expectorant effects.

KNOT WEED

Giant knotweed

A tall and robust perennial plant that can grow up to 4 meters in height and has large leaves and dense clusters of white flowers.

Where can you find it	Native to Japan, China, and Siberia, but now also found in Europe and North America.
Edible parts	Young shoots and leaves can be used in salads, stir-fries, or cooked vegetables.
Flavor	The shoots have a tart, lemony flavor.
Caution	Contains high levels of oxalic acid, which can cause kidney stones in susceptible individuals.
Use	Used in traditional medicine to treat various ailments such as respiratory problems, gastrointestinal disorders, and inflammation.
Nutritional value	Rich in vitamins A and C and minerals such as potassium and calcium.

Himalayan knotweed

A perennial herb that can grow up to 1 meter in height and has reddish-brown stems and lance-shaped leaves.

Where can you find it	Native to the Himalayan region, but also found in North America, Europe, and Australia.
Edible parts	Young shoots and leaves can be used in salads, stir-fries, or cooked vegetables.
Flavor	The shoots have a slightly sour taste.
Caution	It can be invasive and difficult to control.
Use	Used in traditional medicine to treat various ailments such as fever, diarrhea, and inflammation.
Nutritional value	Rich in vitamins A and C and minerals such as potassium and calcium.

Japanese knotweed

A tall and fast-growing perennial plant that can reach up to 3 meters in height and has reddish-brown stems and large, heart-shaped leaves.

Where can you find it	Native to Japan, but now also found in Europe and North America.
Edible parts	Young shoots can be used in salads, stir-fries, or cooked vegetables.
Flavor	The shoots have a sour, tangy flavor.
Caution	It can be invasive and difficult to control.
Use	Used in traditional medicine to treat various ailments such as cardiovascular disease, gastrointestinal disorders, and inflammation.
Nutritional value	Rich in vitamins A and C and minerals such as potassium and calcium.

Mexican bamboo

A perennial plant that can grow up to 2 meters in height and has greenish-brown stems and heart-shaped leaves.

Where can you find it	Native to Japan, China, and Korea, but now also found in North America and Europe.
Edible parts	Young shoots can be used in salads, stir-fries, or cooked vegetables.
Flavor	The shoots have a slightly sour taste.
Caution	It can be invasive and difficult to control.
Use	Used in traditional medicine to treat various ailments such as inflammation, fever, and skin disorders.
Nutritional value	Rich in vitamins A and C and minerals such as potassium and calcium.

Pink knotweed

A perennial herb that can grow up to 60 cm in height and has small, pinkish-white flowers and oval-shaped leaves.

Where can you find it	Native to China, but now also found in North America, Europe, and Australia.
Edible parts	Young leaves and shoots can be used in salads or as cooked vegetables.
Flavor	The leaves have a slightly bitter taste.
Caution	It can be invasive and difficult to control.
Use	Used in traditional medicine to treat various ailments such as coughs, colds, and fevers.
Nutritional value	Rich in vitamins A and C and minerals such as calcium and iron.

Prostrate knotweed

A low-growing annual plant that can reach up to 30 cm in height and has small, pinkish-white flowers and lance-shaped leaves.

Where can you find it	Found in many parts of the world, including North America, Europe, and Asia.
Edible parts	Young leaves and shoots can be used in salads or as cooked vegetable.
Flavor	The leaves have a slightly sour taste.
Caution	It can be invasive and difficult to control.
Use	Used in traditional medicine to treat various ailments such as urinary tract infections, gastrointestinal disorders, and skin disorders.
Nutritional value	Rich in vitamins A and C and minerals such as calcium and iron.

This chapter explored 60 edible wild plants with unique flavors and nutritional profiles. By familiarizing ourselves with these plants, we can expand our culinary horizons, add new flavors and textures to our diets, and reap the health benefits of consuming fresh, nutrient-dense foods.

It's important to remember that foraging for wild plants should always be done with care and respect for the natural environment. We should only harvest plants that we can identify positively and always avoid toxic or potentially harmful plants. It's also a good practice to leave plenty of plants behind for wildlife and other foragers.

So why not try something new? The next time you're out for a walk or hike, keep your eyes peeled for some of the wild plants we've discussed and see what culinary delights nature has in store. By incorporating wild plants into our diets, we can reconnect with nature, appreciate its abundance, and deepen our understanding of the natural world.

BOOK 4: IDENTIFYING INEDIBLE WILD PLANTS

CHAPTER ONE

IDENTIFYING TOXIC PLANTS
*

Plants can be a source of health, beauty, and nutrition, but they can also be harmful. Some plants include toxins that can affect people in different ways, ranging from minor skin irritations to serious poisoning and even death. This makes knowing how to spot hazardous plants and staying away from them crucial. What are the primary traits that can determine whether a plant is poisonous, then? Observe the following warning signs:

1. A plant's morphology, or physical features, can offer significant hints concerning its toxicity. While there are some exceptions, many hazardous plants have distinguishing characteristics that make them simple to spot. For instance:

• **Vibrantly colored flowers or foliage**: Some toxic plants have vivid red, yellow, or purple flowers or leaves. These hues may be visually pleasing, but they can also serve as a warning that the plant is poisonous. For instance, the ricin-containing seeds and brightly colored leaves of the castor oil plant (Ricinus communis) are poisonous and lethal.

• **Sharp spines or thorns**: Many poisonous plants have these features, which can hurt both people and animals physically. For instance, the prickly stems and leaves of the bull nettle (Cnidoscolus texanus) can result in severe rash and skin blisters.

• **Bitter or unappealing flavor or aroma**: Some poisonous plants have a flavor or aroma that is powerful or unpleasant and can dissuade animals and people from ingesting them. For instance, the poison hemlock (Conium maculatum) has a peculiar smell that is similar to the smell of mouse urine.

• **Unusual growth patterns**: Some hazardous plants stand out from other plants due to their distinctive development patterns. The jimsonweed (Datura stramonium), for instance, has huge, trumpet-shaped flowers that develop on a spiky stem. Toxic alkaloids found in the plant have the potential to cause hallucinations and other harmful side effects.

• Although plant morphology can be useful in identifying poisonous plants, it is vital to remember that it is not infallible. Some non-toxic plants may have toxic sections, and some toxic plants may resemble non-toxic plants in appearance. As a result, if you have any doubts regarding the safety of a particular plant, you should always proceed with caution and seek the advice of a professional.

• **Growing circumstances**: Some poisonous plants favor particular habitats for growth. For instance, some plants that grow in wetlands or close to water sources may be poisonous because they take up and store poisons from the soil or water around them.

2. Location is another crucial aspect to take into account when selecting poisonous plants. It's important to be aware of the harmful plants that are common in your area because different parts of the planet have more dangerous plants than others. People who reside in rural or distant places, where they might frequently come into contact with hazardous plants, should pay particular attention to this.

One typical hazardous plant in North America is poison ivy (Toxicodendron radicans). It can result in a severe rash and skin blisters and grows as a vine or shrub. The hazardous plant known as giant hogweed, or Heracleum mantegazzianum, is also frequently found in Europe and Asia. It can reach a height of 14 feet and leave serious burns and skin sores.

In addition to being aware of the poisonous plants in your neighborhood, it's critical to exercise caution when visiting other places. For those who want to go hiking, camping, or foraging for wild flora, this is very significant. It's crucial to conduct your homework and speak with local experts before visiting a new place to identify any potentially poisonous flora.

When identifying poisonous plants, geographic location is a crucial component to take into account. Your chance of getting into touch with toxic plants and experiencing their negative effects can be reduced by being informed of the dangerous plants in your area and taking measures while visiting unfamiliar places.

3. Another crucial aspect to take into account when identifying poisonous plants is their usage history. Despite the fact that many plants have been used for millennia in traditional medicine, this does not necessarily guarantee that they are safe to eat. Many plants that have historically been used as medicines can be harmful if ingested in big doses or prepared incorrectly.

For instance, foxglove (Digitalis purpurea) has been used to treat cardiac issues for generations. Digitalis, a powerful cardiac glycoside found in the plant, can be toxic when ingested in excessive doses. Similar to the castor bean, which also contains the lethal toxin ricin, the castor bean (Ricinus communis) has been employed in traditional medicine for its laxative effects.

It's crucial to keep in mind that just because a plant has been used for generations in traditional medicine doesn't guarantee it's safe to eat. Traditional treatments might not have undergone thorough scientific testing but rather may have been created through trial and error.

Some hazardous plants have also been used recreationally in addition to being utilized as traditional medicine. For instance, the plant known as jimsonweed

(Datura stramonium) has long been used as a hallucinogen. The plant does, however, contain a number of poisonous alkaloids that can result in delirium, confusion, and even death.

When identifying poisonous plants, the history of use is a crucial factor to take into account. It's crucial to keep in mind that just because a plant has been used for generations in traditional medicine doesn't necessarily guarantee that it is safe to eat. You can reduce your risk of coming into touch with hazardous plants and experiencing their negative effects by being aware of the potential risks connected to both traditional treatments and recreational plant use.

4. When identifying poisonous plants, the impact a plant has on people and animals is undoubtedly the most important factor to take into account. The signs of plant poisoning can vary greatly depending on the plant and the type of exposure. Skin irritations including rashes or blisters, nausea, vomiting, diarrhoea, breathing difficulties, convulsions, and even death are some of the most typical symptoms.

It's crucial to remember that depending on a number of variables, such as the type of plant, the age and health of the person or animal, and the amount of exposure, the severity of these symptoms might differ. In certain instances, a small amount of a toxic plant can result in severe symptoms, whilst in other instances, a larger amount may be required to have any discernible effects.

Additionally, a plant's toxicity levels may vary among its many components. For instance, a plant's leaves could be more toxic than its stem or blooms. The degree of toxicity may also be impacted by the preparation technique. Some plants could be poisonous when eaten raw but safe when cooked.

It's crucial to remember that a plant may have distinct effects on people and animals. For instance, a plant that is hazardous to humans may not always be toxic to animals, and the opposite is also true. This means that while identifying hazardous plants, it is crucial to take into account the possible risks to humans and animals.

In conclusion, determining a plant's toxicity depends on how it affects both people and animals. Symptoms of plant toxicity can vary greatly and can be mild to severe. Understanding the possible dangers posed by various plants and the variables that may influence their level of toxicity is crucial. Your risk of an encounter with hazardous plants can be reduced with knowledge of their impacts.

In the end, being educated about the plants in your environment and employing caution and good judgment when foraging or utilizing plants as medicine are the greatest ways to avoid dangerous plants. Always err on the side of caution and stay away from a plant if you have any doubts about it.

CHAPTER TWO
THE MOST POISONOUS PLANTS
*

Our natural ecosystem depends on plants because they give us food, shelter, and oxygen. But some plants can be extremely dangerous and even deadly if consumed. These plants' poisonous substances are mostly utilized as a kind of protection against predators like insects and animals. Depending on the particular plant and the quantity taken, the symptoms brought on by ingesting poisonous plants might vary in severity. Occasionally, a small number of berries or leaves might result in serious symptoms or even death. The effects of poisoning can differ from person to person and depend on a number of variables, including age, weight, and general health.

Mild stomach discomfort to serious neurological and cardiovascular consequences can all be signs of plant poisoning. As a result of consuming poisonous herbs, nausea, vomiting, diarrhoea, and stomach discomfort are frequent side effects. Confusion, hallucinations, convulsions, an irregular pulse, and respiratory failure are further symptoms. Poisonous plant consumption can, in extreme circumstances, result in unconsciousness and death.

Knowing how to spot hazardous plants and staying away from them is crucial. Commonly found in gardens, parks, and the outdoors are some of the most poisonous plants. Children and animals are particularly susceptible to plant poisoning, therefore it's important to warn them about the risks of eating plants and keep them away from potentially harmful vegetation.

1. Atropa belladonna, a plant that is native to Europe, North Africa, and Western Asia, is extremely toxic. Other names for it are Devil's Berries and Belladonna. Shiny black, cherry-like berries that are produced by the plant are extremely dangerous and should never be swallowed. The deadly alkaloids atropine and scopolamine, which are present throughout the entire plant, including the leaves and stems, can be consumed in large enough doses to be lethal. Deadly Nightshade poisoning can cause severe and quick-onset symptoms. Even a small amount of berries can cause a variety of symptoms, such as dry mouth, blurred vision, trouble swallowing, confusion, hallucinations, and seizures. Within a few hours of consumption, these symptoms can appear, and if they aren't treated right away, they could be fatal.

The central nervous system is poisonous to atropine and scopolamine, and their side effects can be severe. Consuming Deadly Nightshade can, in extreme situations, cause respiratory failure and death. The plant can be harmful in even tiny doses, especially to kids who could be drawn to glossy berries. It's vital to remember that atropine and scopolamine have both been used medicinally throughout history and are still utilized today. To reduce the risk of poisoning, these substances are used in precisely measured amounts and under medical supervision.

A severely dangerous plant that needs to be avoided at all costs is the deadly nightshade. The symptoms of poisoning can be severe and have long-lasting repercussions or even result in death. Seek emergency medical assistance if you think you or someone else may have consumed this plant.

2. Originally from Africa, the big plant known as the castor bean (Ricinus communis) is today farmed all over the world. It is frequently utilized for its oil, which has numerous industrial and therapeutic uses. However, ricin, a very poisonous protein that can be lethal if consumed, is present in castor bean seeds.

One of the most potent naturally occurring toxins is ricin, and only a small number of castor beans can have levels of ricin that are fatal to humans. Within a few hours of intake, ricin poisoning symptoms can emerge and include severe vomiting, diarrhea, dehydration, convulsions, and even death. In some situations, the rapid and severe effects of ricin on the organism might result in organ failure and death.

It's crucial to remember that ricin cannot be absorbed via the skin, making plant handling largely risk-free. The poisonous protein can be released from the seeds if they are chewed or crushed, though. Depending on how much of the toxin was consumed, ricin poisoning symptoms might vary, but even small doses can be harmful and need to be treated as a medical emergency.

Avoid using the potentially toxic plant known as castor bean. The seeds contain ricin, a strong poison that, when consumed, can result in serious illness and even death. It's critical to be aware of the risks posed by this plant and to take the necessary precautions to avoid unintentional intake.

3. Conium maculatum, a plant that was once only found in Europe and Asia, is now widespread throughout the world, including North America. Coniine, a powerful toxin found in every part of the plant, can be lethal if consumed even in small doses.

Hemlock poisoning symptoms can manifest quickly, frequently between 30 and 60 minutes after consumption. There may be a variety of symptoms, such as nausea, tremors, muscle aches, breathing problems, and coma. Coniine's effects on the body can be swift and severe, and in rare situations, they can be fatal.

It's crucial to remember that Poison Hemlock can be mistaken for food plants like parsley or wild carrots because of the way its leaves and stems look. In order to prevent ingesting this plant, it is crucial to recognize it.

Poison hemlock is a highly toxic plant that needs to be avoided at all costs, to sum up. The entire plant, including the leaves, stems, and blossoms, are loaded with a toxic substance that, when consumed, can result in severe symptoms and even death. It's critical to be aware of the risks posed by this plant and to take the necessary precautions to avoid unintentional intake.

4. Although it originated in the Mediterranean region, oleander (Nerium oleander) is now widely planted all over the world. The leaves stem, flowers and sap of the oleander plant are all rich in cardiac glycosides, a strong mixture of poisons. If consumed, these poisons can result in severe illness and even death.

The signs of oleander poisoning can differ depending on how much of the toxin was consumed, but they normally show up a few hours after consumption. Abdominal pain, nausea, and vomiting are some of the early signs. More serious symptoms, such as an abnormal heartbeat, convulsions, a coma, and even death, can appear as the poisoning worsens.

It's crucial to remember that oleander poisoning can also result from coming into contact with the plant's sap, which can irritate the skin, and the eyes, and trigger other allergic reactions. Therefore, it's crucial to take the proper safety precautions when handling the plant, such as donning gloves and covering yourself.

The oleander plant is extremely dangerous and ought to be avoided at all costs. Every portion of the plant carries a strong mixture of poisons that, if consumed or encountered, can result in severe illness and even death. It's critical to be informed of the risks posed by this plant and to take the necessary precautions to avoid unintentional intake or contact.

5. Originally from North America, Jimsonweed (Datura stramonium), often known as Devil's Trumpet, is an extremely poisonous plant that is now widespread around the world. The plant includes strong hallucinogens including atropine, scopolamine, and hyoscyamine. Various symptoms, such as delirium, disorientation, agitation, and seizures, can be brought on by these substances.

Depending on how much of the toxin was consumed, Jimsonweed poisoning symptoms can develop 30 minutes to an hour after intake. Small doses of plant ingestion can result in minor symptoms such as dilated pupils, parched mouth, and flushed skin. More severe symptoms, such as hallucinations, delirium, agitation, and seizures, can arise from ingesting larger quantities. Jimsonweed poisoning can be lethal in rare circumstances.

It's crucial to remember that Jimsonweed is occasionally used illicitly as a hallucinogenic drug, but this is exceedingly risky and can result in serious poisoning or even death. It's also crucial to be aware that Jimsonweed can accidentally be consumed if it's mistaken for edible plants like Jerusalem cherry or black nightshade.

Jimsonweed is a severely dangerous plant that needs to be avoided at all costs, to sum up. A variety of strong

hallucinogenic substances found in the plant can produce mild to severe hallucinations. To avoid accidental intake or use as a recreational drug, it is imperative to be aware of the risks posed by this plant and to take the necessary precautions.

6. Foxglove (Digitalis purpurea), a plant that originated in Europe but is now widespread around the world, is extremely poisonous. A complex mixture of cardiac glycosides, including the potent cardiac stimulants digitoxin and digoxin, are present in the plant. Numerous symptoms, such as irregular heartbeats, nausea, vomiting, dizziness, seizures, and even death, can be brought on by these substances.

Depending on how much of the toxin was consumed, Foxglove poisoning symptoms might manifest as soon as a few hours after intake. Early signs may include nausea, vomiting, pain in the abdomen, and diarrhea. More serious symptoms, including abnormal heartbeats, disorientation, seizures, and coma, might develop as the poisoning worsens. Foxglove poisoning can be lethal in extreme circumstances.

It's crucial to remember that foxglove is occasionally used medicinally to treat heart issues, but this should only be done with a doctor's approval. Digitalis has a very low therapeutic dose, and improper usage of the plant can quickly lead to an overdose.

To sum up, foxglove is a dangerous plant that needs to be avoided at all costs. A strong mixture of cardiac glycosides found in the plant can produce a range of symptoms, from moderate to severe. It's critical to be aware of the risks posed by this plant and to take the necessary precautions to avoid unintentional intake. If you need to utilize foxglove for medical purposes, seek the advice of a doctor before doing so.

7. One of the most lethal plants in North America is water hemlock (Cicuta douglasii). It is a perennial plant that thrives in moist places like stream banks, marshes, and swamps. Cicutoxin, a very toxic substance found in the plant, may severely poison both people and animals.

Any component of the water hemlock plant can be fatal to consume, and death can happen shortly after consumption. Poisoning symptoms, such as nausea, vomiting, stomach pain, tremors, convulsions, respiratory failure, and coma, can manifest anywhere between 15 minutes and several hours after intake. Since the symptoms might be severe, hospitalization and supportive care may be necessary.

Due to its resemblance in appearance to edible plants like wild carrots and parsley, water hemlock can occasionally be mistaken for them. A hollow stem with purple spots, umbrella-like clusters of white blooms, and finely divided leaves with sharply toothed edges are just a few of the plant's distinguishing characteristics. To prevent unintentional intake, it is crucial to recognize the plant.

Water Hemlock is a highly hazardous plant that needs to be avoided at all costs, to sum up. Cicutoxin, a very toxic substance found in the plant, may severely poison both people and animals. To prevent unintentional ingestion, it is imperative to correctly identify the plant. Consult a doctor right away if you think you or someone else may have consumed water hyssop.

8. A coniferous tree found in both Europe and North America is the yew (Taxus baccata). The yew is one of the most poisonous plants in the world, despite being a common decorative plant because of its lovely foliage and berries. Taxine, a highly poisonous alkaloid found in yew leaves, seeds, and bark, can lead to serious poisoning in both humans and animals.

Yew is dangerous to consume in any amount. The symptoms of poisoning, which include vomiting, diarrhea, abdominal discomfort, an erratic heartbeat, convulsions, and death, can manifest right away or take a while to do so. There may not always be any symptoms prior to a fatal collapse.

Yew has been employed as a poison since ancient times, and its deadly qualities have long been known. Although some conventional medicines also contain yew, their usage is not advised due to their toxicity.

The risks posed by yew must be understood, and proper measures must be taken. Pets should not be let around the plant, and children should be trained not to eat the berries. Gardeners and landscapers working with yew should wear safety gloves and wash their hands thoroughly after handling the plant.

It is critical to get medical assistance right away in the event of consumption. To remove the poison, the doctor may induce vomiting or give activated charcoal; supportive care may also be provided, such as IV fluids and vital sign monitoring. Hospitalization might be necessary for extreme circumstances to treat symptoms and stop organ failure.

Yew plants are extremely toxic, and eating any portion of one could be lethal. Taxine, a very toxic alkaloid found in the leaves, seeds, and bark, can seriously poison both people and animals. When working with yew, it is crucial to take the proper safety procedures and seek medical help right once if ingested.

9. Originally from South America, the flowering plant known as the angel's trumpet (Brugmansia spp.) is now widely grown as an ornamental plant around the world. The plant is among the most poisonous to humans that is known and prized for its big, trumpet-shaped blooms and potent aroma.

Scopolamine, atropine, and hyoscyamine are among the alkaloids found in Angel's Trumpet's leaves and flowers. These alkaloids can cause a variety of symptoms, such as hallucinations, delirium, disorientation, and paralysis, and they have strong effects on the central nervous system.

Angel's Trumpet can be lethal in large doses, especially to children and animals. Symptoms of poisoning, such as nausea, vomiting, dry mouth, impaired vision, fast heartbeat, fever, and seizures, might arise suddenly. In extreme situations, a coma and death are possible.

When working with Angel's Trumpet, it is crucial to follow the proper safety procedures, which include donning protective gear and clothes, washing your hands completely after handling the plant, and using gloves. If the plant is cultivated in a public space, it should be properly labeled and kept away from children and pets.

To sum up, Angel's Trumpet is a very poisonous plant that can result in a variety of symptoms like hallucinations, delirium, disorientation, and paralysis. Using the plant safely requires following the necessary measures because ingesting big amounts can be dangerous. Angel's Trumpet should not be swallowed without prompt medical assistance.

10. A common decorative plant called lily of the valley (Convallaria majalis) blooms in the spring with tiny, fragrant white flowers. The plant is stunning, but it also has strong toxins that are dangerous to both people and animals. The cardiac glycosides in the lily of the valley, such as sconvallatoxin and convallarin, are the principal poisonous elements. Numerous symptoms, such as nausea, vomiting, diarrhea, abdominal discomfort, headaches, dizziness, confusion, visual abnormalities, irregular heartbeats, and seizures, can be brought on by these substances. In extreme circumstances, consuming a lot of the plant can cause death by coma, respiratory failure, and coma.

Due to their potential attraction to the plant's vibrant berries and leaves, children and pets are especially susceptible to the harmful effects of the lily of the valley. Ingesting even a small amount of the plant, such as one or two leaves or berries, might result in serious symptoms.

Lily of the Valley must be handled carefully and kept away from children and animals in order to prevent unintentional poisoning. If you have a plant in your garden, wash your hands thoroughly after dealing with it and wear gloves when handling it. It might be preferable to completely avoid planting lilies in the valley if you have young children or pets.

As a result, lily of the valley is a stunning but dangerous plant that contains cardiac glycosides that can result in a variety of symptoms like nausea, vomiting, diarrhea, irregular heartbeats, and seizures. It is crucial to seek medical assistance right once someone has consumed the plant because huge doses can be lethal. To avoid unintentional poisoning, the plant must be handled carefully and kept away from children and animals.

CHAPTER THREE
BE CAREFUL WHAT YOU FOUND
*

It is crucial to understand that some plants can be extremely hazardous and even fatal if consumed. Sadly, certain deadly plants can be mistaken for edible ones, which might result in unforeseen dangers. In order to help you recognize and steer clear of some of the key hazardous plants that can be confused for edible plants, we'll go through them in this chapter. You can enjoy the natural world with confidence and safety if you are knowledgeable about these plants.

1. Poison hemlock (Conium maculatum): This plant, which resembles a wild carrot or parsley, can make you sick and put you in a coma if you eat it. It can also produce tremors, muscle weakness, respiratory failure, and coma.

2. Water hemlock (Cicuta douglasii): This plant, which is sometimes confused with Queen Anne's lace or wild parsnip, can make you nauseous, throw up, have stomach pain, have seizures, have respiratory failure, and go into a coma if you eat it.

3. Deadly nightshade (Atropa belladonna): This plant, which looks similar to blueberries or blackberries, is poisonous and can be consumed to cause hallucinations, convulsions, dry mouth, impaired vision, difficulty swallowing, confusion, and difficulty concentrating.

4. Jimsonweed (Datura stramonium): This plant is sometimes mistaken for a type of edible nightshade and, if consumed, can result in delirium, confusion, agitation, and convulsions.

5. Poison ivy (Toxicodendron radicans): This plant, which is sometimes confused with Boston ivy or Virginia creeper, can result in an itchy, unpleasant rash when handled or swallowed.

6. False morel (Gyromitra esculenta): This plant, which is sometimes confused for real morels, can make you sick, make you throw up, make your stomach hurt, and even make you die.

7. Yew (Taxus baccata): This plant, which looks a lot like holly or conifers, if consumed, can result in death. It can also cause vomiting, diarrhea, stomach pain, irregular heartbeat, convulsions, and vomiting.

BOOK 5: THE FORAGER'S CALENDAR

INTRODUCTION

Finding natural plants can be a pleasant and enjoyable activity, especially if you don't have to go far. You can cultivate some of the best forage plants in your garden! The greatest wild plants to forage in your garden will be the topic of this chapter. So that you may begin your foraging adventure right away, we'll highlight plants that need little area and are simple to grow.

This chapter has all you need, whether you're seeking herbs to spice your food or edible flowers to garnish your salads. We've compiled a list of the top wild plants that may be grown rapidly in a backyard garden without taking up as much room or demanding as much upkeep as larger trees or shrubs might. You may have a constant supply of fresh wild plants for foraging at your disposal with a little work and attention.

So let's get started if you're prepared to learn about the greatest wild plants to forage in your garden.

CHAPTER ONE

JANUARY
*

Foragers may find January difficult, particularly in colder areas. However, many plants can still be foraged at this time of year, especially in areas with warmer climates. In this post, some of the greatest wild plants for foraging in January will be discussed.

1. Rosehips: The fruit of the rose plant, rosehips are usually plucked in the late summer or early fall. They can survive the winter on the plant, though, and can be harvested in January. These little, oblong fruits can be used to produce tea, jams, or even wine and are rich in vitamin C.

2. Nettles: Although less plentiful in the winter, nettles provide a year-round source of nutrition. However, nettle shoots that are just beginning to grow in protected locations may be seen in January if you know where to look. These can be picked and substituted for spinach in dishes like soups and stews.

3. Chickweed: Chickweed is a widespread weed that may be found all over the world. It is a lovely shrub with tiny white blossoms that is well-known for its therapeutic benefits. It can be cooked as green or eaten raw in salads. Chickweed may be grown in sheltered places or urban settings in January.

4. Dandelion: Another widespread weed in many regions of the world is the dandelion. Their sharply serrated leaves and vivid yellow blossoms are well renowned for them. Young dandelion leaves may be visible poking out from the ground in January. These can be cooked green or eaten raw in salads.

5. Wintergreen: Wintergreen is a low-growing plant that can be found in colder climates. It is used for flavoring confectionery and gum due to its characteristic minty taste. The leaves can be collected and used to flavor desserts or to brew tea. Under a layer of snow in January, wintergreen may be growing.

6. Haws: Often ignored as wild food, haws are the fruit of the hawthorn tree. They are tiny, vivid red berries that can be used to produce jams or sauces and are high in vitamin C. Haws may still be on the tree in January, though they might be a little past their peak.

Pine needles are a good source of vitamin C and can be brewed into tea or used to season foods. Young pine shoots may start to emerge from the ground in January. Similar to pine needles, these can be collected and used.

In conclusion, foragers may find January to be difficult, yet a number of plants can still be found foraging throughout this month. So, venture outside and begin your exploration! Even in the dead of winter, you can enjoy a fresh supply of wild plants if you know what to look for and where to seek.

CHAPTER TWO

FEBRUARY
*

Like January, foragers may have difficulties in February. However, many plants can still be foraged at this time of year, especially in areas with warmer climates. The greatest natural plants to forage in February will be covered in this post.

1. Birch sap: Birch trees begin to generate sap in the late winter, which can be collected and utilized as a cool beverage. Since ancient times, birch sap has been employed in traditional medicine as a natural source of vitamins and minerals. Make a small hole in the birch tree's trunk and catch the drips in a container to harvest the sap. Although birch sap is tastiest when taken immediately, it can be kept in a refrigerator for up to a week.

2. Cleavers (Galium aparine): Also known as goosegrass, cleavers are a widespread weed that may be found all over the world. Their leaves are notorious for being sticky and clinging to both flesh and clothing. Young cleaver shoots may start to emerge from the ground in February. These can be picked and substituted for spinach in dishes like soups and stews. Additionally used to treat skin disorders and bladder issues, cleavers are known for their therapeutic qualities.

3. Hawthorn berries: The berry of the hawthorn tree is frequently disregarded as a source of wild food. They are tiny, vibrant red berries that are packed with antioxidants and may be used to make jam, sauces, and even wine. Hawthorn berries might still be on the tree in February, though they might be a little past their best. Before using the berries in cooking, make sure to remove the seeds because they can be harmful if consumed in big quantities.

4. Garlic mustard, also known as Alliaria petiolata, is a biennial plant that is native to Europe and Asia but has spread aggressively around the world. It can be used as a spice for meats and can be used in salads, soups, and other dishes because of its characteristic garlic-like flavor. Young garlic mustard leaves may start to emerge from the ground in February. Similar to other leafy greens, these can be picked and prepared for use.

5. Wintergreen (Gaultheria procumbens): This low-growing plant is indigenous to colder climates. It is used for flavoring confectionery and gum due to its characteristic minty taste. The leaves can be collected and used to flavor desserts or to brew tea. Under a layer of snow in February, wintergreen may be growing.

6. Spruce tips can be harvested in late winter or early spring. Spruce tips are the fresh growth at the ends of spruce branches. They have a distinct, citrus-like flavor and are rich in vitamin C. Spruce tips can be used to season meats and create tea, and syrups. Pluck the fresh growth at the branch's end and trim away any woody or brown areas to harvest spruce tips.

While foraging may not be at its best in February, a number of plants are still accessible. So, take a basket, gear up, and venture outside to discover February's untamed landscapes. Even in the dead of winter, you can find new supplies of wild plants if you know what to search for and where to seek.

CHAPTER THREE

MARCH

As winter gradually ends, spring breathes new vitality and vigor into the natural world. As the seasons change, so do the wild plants that are available for foraging in March. The following list includes some of the top wild plants to harvest now:

Nettles (Urtica dioica) is a nutrient-rich wild plant that can be found all over the world. Since ancient times, nettles have been utilized in traditional medicine because of their high vitamin and mineral content. Young nettle shoots can be picked in the early spring and used in soups, stews, or in place of spinach. They wear gloves during harvesting because the hairs are also renowned for stinging.

2. Dandelion, or Taraxacum officinale, is a widespread weed throughout much of the world. Dandelion leaves can be picked in the early spring and cooked or used in salads. Dandelion leaves have a mildly bitter flavor and are rich in vitamins and minerals. In order to generate a beverage similar to coffee, dandelion roots can also be gathered and roasted.

3. Wild garlic (Allium ursinum): Also known as ramsons, wild garlic is a plant that grows wild in wooded places all over Europe and Asia. Wild garlic leaves are gathered in the early spring and used as flavoring for meats, soups, and stews. Wild garlic is rich in vitamins and minerals and has a potent flavor.

4. Elderberry (Sambucus nigra): In the late summer and early fall, elderberry is a plant that bears tiny, dark purple berries. Elderberry buds can be collected in the early spring to make a tea that is rich in antioxidants and vitamin C. In the spring, elderberry blooms can also be collected to make a fragrant and savory cordial.

5. Wild leeks (Allium tricoccum): Native to eastern North America, wild leeks are often referred to as ramps. Wild leeks are rich in vitamins and minerals and have a strong onion flavor. The leaves of wild leeks can be gathered in the early spring and used in soups, stews, or as a flavoring for meats.

6. Chickweed (Stellaria media) is a widespread weed that may be found all over the world. Chickweed has a moderate, somewhat sweet flavor and is rich in vitamins and minerals. Young chickweed shoots can be collected in the early spring and added to salads or used as a garnish.

Foraging may not be at its best in March, but a number of wild plants can still be collected at this time of year. Get outside, stroll through the fields and woods, and learn about the marvels of March foraging. Knowing what to look for and where to locate it will enable you to regularly consume a supply of nourishing and delectable wild plants.

CHAPTER FOUR

APRIL

*

The month of April is a vibrant one for new growth and activity in the natural world. This is the time of year when a lot of wild plants start to come out of their winter hibernation, giving foragers a ton of delicious and nourishing options. Some of the greatest wild plants to harvest in April are listed below:

1. Wild asparagus (Asparagus officinalis): In many regions of the world, wild asparagus is a tasty and nutrient-rich wild plant. April is the time of year when wild asparagus shoots first appear from the ground and can be collected for salads, stir-fries, or as a side dish. Wild asparagus has a little bitter flavor and is rich in vitamins and minerals, especially vitamin K.

2. Wild strawberry (Fragaria vesca): Around the world, meadows and forested regions are home to sweet and tasty fruit. In April, the first wild strawberry plants blossom, and the fruit appears soon after. Wild strawberries can be used to make jams and jellies, eaten fresh, and are rich in vitamin C and antioxidants.

3. Stinging nettle (Urtica dioica) is a widespread wild plant that can be found all over the world. Since ancient times, nettles have been utilized in traditional medicine because they are rich in vitamins and minerals. Nettle leaves can be picked in April and substituted for spinach in soups and stews. When harvesting, take sure to use gloves because the stinging hairs might be uncomfortable.

4. Wild garlic mustard (Alliaria petiolata) is a plant that grows wild all over the world. Garlic mustard has a flavor that is distinctly garlic-like and is rich in vitamins and minerals. Wild garlic mustard leaves can be gathered in April and used as flavoring for meats, pesto, and salads.

5. Watercress (Nasturtium officinale) is a tasty and nutrient-rich wild plant that may be discovered in freshwater streams and rivers all over the world. Watercress has a somewhat peppery flavor and is rich in vitamins and minerals, especially vitamin C. In April, watercress leaves can be collected and used as a garnish or in salads and soups.

6. Ramp (Allium tricoccum): Native to eastern North America, ramps are also referred to as wild leeks. Ramps sprout from the ground in April, and their leaves can be picked and used as a spice for meats, stews, and soups. Ramps are rich in vitamins and minerals and have a flavor that strongly resembles an onion.

7. Wild violets (Viola odorata): Wild violets are fragrant and colorful plants that grow wild throughout much of the world. Wild violet blooms and leaves can be collected in April and added to salads or used as a garnish. Wild violets have a sweet, flowery flavor and a high antioxidant content.

In conclusion, a variety of wild plants thaw out in April, offering foragers scrumptious and nourishing options. Get outside to appreciate the delights of April foraging by strolling around the fields and woodlands. Knowing what to look for and where to locate it will enable you to regularly consume a source of delectable and nutritious wild plants.

CHAPTER 5

MAY
*

May is a month of growth and regeneration in the natural world, making it a great time for foragers to discover the variety of wild plants that are readily available. The leaves, flowers, and fruits of many untamed plants are in full bloom and ready for harvesting. Some of the top wild plants to harvest in May are listed below:

1. Dandelion (Taraxacum officinale): Despite being a widespread wild plant that is frequently regarded as a weed, dandelion is actually a highly nutritious and adaptable plant that may be used in a variety of ways. For instance, vitamin K and antioxidants are abundant in dandelion. The dandelion's yellow blooms start to blossom in May, and the leaves can be picked for salads, soups, and sautés.

2. Wild garlic (Allium ursinum): Also known as ramsons, wild garlic is a plant that grows wild throughout Europe and Asia. Wild garlic is rich in vitamins and minerals, especially vitamin C, and has a strong, pungent flavor. Wild garlic leaves and blooms can be collected in May and used as flavoring for meats, salads, and soups.

3. Elderflower (Sambucus nigra): Found in many parts of the world, elderflower is a fragrant and tasty wild plant. Elderflower has a pleasant, flowery flavor and a high antioxidant content. The elder plant's blooms can be picked in May and added to syrups, cordials, or sweets as a flavoring.

4. Wild lettuce (Lactuca serriola) is a plant that grows wild in many regions of the world, including North America, Asia, and Europe. Wild lettuce leaves can be collected in May and added to salads or used in place of lettuce in sandwiches and wraps. Wild lettuce has a little bitter flavor and is rich in vitamins and minerals, especially vitamin C.

5. Red clover (Trifolium pratense): Commonly found in fields and meadows, red clover is a type of wild plant. Red clover flowers can be picked in May and added to drinks, syrups, and garnishes. Antioxidant-rich red clover has a pleasant, flowery flavor.

6. Sweet cicely (Myrrhis odorata): This wild plant is indigenous to Asia and Europe. Sweet cicely is rich in vitamins and minerals, especially vitamin C, and has a sweet, anise-like flavor. The sweet cicely plant's leaves and blooms can be collected in May and eaten in salads or as a flavoring for meats.

7. Wild strawberry (Fragaria vesca): Around the world, meadows and woodland places are home to delicious and flavorful fruit. Wild strawberries are rich in antioxidants and vitamin C. The first wild strawberry fruits start to ripen in May and can be picked to make jams, jellies, or to eat straight from the ground.

In conclusion, foragers have a variety of scrumptious and nourishing wild plants to choose from since May is a month of growth and rejuvenation in the natural world. Get outside to appreciate the beauties of May foraging by strolling around the fields and woodlands. Knowing what to look for and where to locate it will enable you to regularly consume a source of delectable and nutritious wild plants.

CHAPTER SIX

JUNE
*

Foragers have plenty to choose from in June since many wild plants are in full bloom and their fruits and berries are ready to be picked. Some of the top wild plants to harvest in June are listed below:

1. Urtica dioica, sometimes known as stinging nettle, is a natural plant that grows all over the world. Contrary to its name, stinging nettle is very nutrient-rich and abundant in vitamins, minerals, and iron. The stinging nettle plant's leaves can be picked in June and used in teas, soups, and recipes in place of spinach.

2. Sambucus nigra, also known as elderberry, is a tasty and nourishing wild plant that grows all over the world. The elder plant's berries start to ripen in June, at which point you can pick them and use them to make syrups, jams, or flavor sweets. Elderberries taste sweet and delicious and are rich in antioxidants.

3. Red raspberry (Rubus idaeus): In many parts of the world, red raspberry is a delicious and flavorful wild fruit. The first red raspberries start to ripen around June, at which point they can be collected and eaten fresh or used to make jams and jellies. Red raspberries are rich in antioxidants and vitamin C.

4. Wild yarrow (Achillea millefolium) is a plant that is indigenous to Europe and Asia. Yarrow is rich in antioxidants and has a bitter, potent flavor. The yarrow plant's leaves and blooms can be picked in June and used as seasoning for meats, salads, and beverages.

5. Wild strawberries (Fragaria vesca) are a sweet and tasty fruit that may be found all over the world in meadows and woodland regions. Wild strawberries are rich in antioxidants and vitamin C. The wild strawberry season is in full force in June, and you may pick them to put in jams and jellies or just enjoy them straight up.

6. Red clover is a common natural plant that can be seen in fields and meadows. Its scientific name is Trifolium pratense. Red clover flowers can be picked in June and added to drinks, syrups, or as a garnish. Antioxidant-rich red clover has a pleasant, flowery flavor.

7. Chicory (Cichorium intybus) is a plant that grows wild all over the world. The chicory plant's leaves and flowers can be picked in June and used in salads or as a substitute for coffee. Chicory is abundant in antioxidants and has a little bitter flavor.

8. Wild carrot (Daucus carota) is a plant that is indigenous to Europe and Asia and is also referred to as Queen Anne's Lace. Wild carrot is rich in vitamins and minerals, including vitamin A, and has a pleasant, flowery flavor. The wild carrot plant's blooms can be picked in June and added to salads or used as a garnish.

In conclusion, June offers foragers a wealth of scrumptious and nourishing wild plants. Knowing what to look for and where to locate it will enable you to regularly consume a source of delectable and nutritious wild plants. Get outside to appreciate the delights of June foraging by strolling around the fields and woodlands.

CHAPTER SEVEN

JULY
*

With numerous wild plants in full bloom and their fruits and berries available for picking, July is another month of abundance for foragers. Some of the greatest wild plants to harvest in July are listed below:

1. Blackberry (Rubus fruticosus): In many regions of the world, blackberries are a sweet and juicy wild fruit. They include lots of antioxidants and vitamin C. Blackberry bushes are in full bloom and ready to harvest their fruits in July. Blackberries can be consumed fresh or added to jams and jellies.

2. Malva sylvestris, often known as common mallow, is a plant that grows wild all over the world. The common mallow plant's leaves and blooms can be picked in July and substituted for spinach in salads and soups. The vitamin A content of common mallow is exceptionally high.

3. Wild thyme (Thymus serpyllum) is a tasty and aromatic wild herb found in rocky, arid regions all over the world. Wild thyme is rich in antioxidants and has a pleasant, earthy flavor. The wild thyme plant's leaves and blooms can be collected in July and used as flavoring for meats, soups, and drinks.

4. The wild plant known as meadowsweet, or Filipendula ulmaria, is indigenous to Europe and Asia. Meadowsweet is rich in antioxidants and has a sweet, floral flavor. The meadowsweet plant's blooms can be picked in July and added to teas, syrups, or desserts as a flavoring.

5. Redcurrants (Ribes rubrum) are a tasty and tart wild fruit that is found all over the world. They include lots of antioxidants and vitamin C. Redcurrant bushes are in full flower and ready to harvest their fruits in July. Redcurrants can be eaten fresh or added to jams and jellies.

6. Wild marjoram (Origanum vulgare) is a herb that grows wild all over the world. The wild marjoram plant's leaves and blossoms can be collected in July and used as a spice for meats, soups, and beverages. Wild marjoram is rich in antioxidants and has a spicy, aromatic flavor.

7. Chicory (Cichorium intybus) is a plant that grows wild all over the world. The chicory plant's leaves and flowers can be picked in July and used in salads or as a substitute for coffee. Chicory is abundant in antioxidants and has a little bitter flavor.

8. The blueberry (Vaccinium myrtillus) is a delicious and flavorful wild fruit that grows all over the world in forested areas and meadows. They taste tart and sweet and are rich in antioxidants. In July, blueberry bushes are in full bloom and ready for plucking. Blueberries can be consumed fresh or added to jams and jellies.

In conclusion, July offers foragers a wealth of scrumptious and nourishing wild plants. Knowing what to look for and where to locate it will enable you to regularly consume a source of delectable and nutritious wild plants. Get outside to appreciate the beauties of July foraging by strolling around the fields and woodlands.

CHAPTER EIGHT
AUGUST
*

A transitional month, August sees the end of summer and the beginning of fall. But foragers can still find many delicious and healthy wild plants in August thanks to the season's abundance. Some of the top wild plants to harvest in August are listed below:

1. Blackcurrants (Ribes nigrum) are a sweet and tasty wild fruit that is grown throughout most of the world. Blackcurrant bushes are in full flower and ready to harvest their fruits in August. Blackcurrants can be eaten fresh or added to jams and jellies. They include lots of antioxidants and vitamin C.

2. Elderberries (Sambucus nigra) are a tart and tasty wild fruit that is grown throughout most of the world. They include lots of antioxidants and vitamin C. Elderberry bushes are in full bloom in August, and their fruits are ready to be picked. Elderberries can be used in wine, syrup, jams, and jellies.

3. Yarrow, or Achillea millefolium, is a common wild herb found around the world. The yarrow plant's leaves and blooms can be collected in August and used to make drinks or season meats. Yarrow is rich in antioxidants and has a mildly bitter flavor.

4. Wild garlic (Allium ursinum) is a tasty and aromatic wild herb that grows in forests and meadows all over the world. Wild garlic is rich in antioxidants and has a pungent, garlicky flavor. The wild garlic plant's leaves can be picked in August and used as a spice for meats, salads, and soups.

5. Wild raspberries (Rubus idaeus) are a sweet and juicy fruit that may be found all over the world in woodland areas and meadows. Raspberries are ready for picking in August when the bushes are in full bloom. Wild raspberries can be consumed fresh or added to jams and jellies. They include lots of antioxidants and vitamin C.

6. Rose hips (Rosa spp.): Rose hips are a type of fruit that grows on wild rose plants and are distributed around the world. Rose hips are rich in antioxidants and vitamin C. Rose hips are ready to be harvested around August and can be used to make tea, syrup, or jelly.

7. Hypericum perforatum, sometimes known as St. John's Wort, is a plant that grows wild in many parts of the world. The St. John's Wort plant's blossoms and leaves can be collected in August and used to make teas or as a seasoning for meats. St. John's Wort is rich in antioxidants and has a mildly bitter flavor.

8. Wild Plum (Prunus spp.): In many regions of the world, wild plums are a sweet and tasty wild fruit. They provide lots of antioxidants and vitamin C in August. Plum trees are currently in full bloom, and their fruits are ready for harvest. Wild plums can be eaten fresh or used to make jams and jellies. They

As a result of many wild plants being in full bloom and having their fruits and berries ready for gathering, August is a great month for foraging. Get outside to appreciate the beauties of August foraging by strolling around the fields and woodlands. Knowing what to look for and where to locate it will enable you to regularly consume a source of delectable and nutritious wild plants.

CHAPTER NINE

SEPTEMBER
*

Autumn officially begins in September, but foragers can still locate a variety of wild plants that are tasty and nutritious throughout this time. Some of the top wild plants to harvest in September are listed below:

1. Apples (Malus spp.): In many places of the world, apples are a common and wholesome wild fruit. Apple trees are in full bloom in September, and their fruits are ready for picking. Aside from being consumed fresh, apples can also be converted into juice or cider, pies, or crisps. They are rich in antioxidants, vitamin C, and fiber.

2. Blackberries (Rubus spp.) are a sweet and tasty wild fruit that grows all over the world in woodland areas and meadows. They include lots of antioxidants and vitamin C. Blackberry bushes are in full bloom and ready to harvest their fruits in September. Blackberries can be consumed fresh or added to jams and jellies.

3. Hawthorn (Crataegus spp.): In many regions of the world, the hawthorn grows wild. The hawthorn tree's fruit, which can be used to produce tea, syrup, or jelly, is ready to be picked in September. Hawthorn is well known for its therapeutic benefits, particularly for enhancing heart health.

4. Honeysuckle (Lonicera spp.) is a wild vine that grows throughout much of the world. Honeysuckle is rich in antioxidants and has a sweet, flowery flavor. The honeysuckle plant's flowers can be picked in September and used to flavor meals or create tea.

5. Rosehips (Rosa spp.): Rosehips are a fruit that grows on wild rose plants and are distributed around the world. Rosehips are rich in antioxidants and vitamin C. Rosehips are ready to be harvested around September and can be used to make tea, syrup, or jelly.

6. Elderberries (Sambucus nigra) are a tasty and tart wild fruit that are grown throughout most of the world. They include lots of antioxidants and vitamin C. Elderberry bushes are in full bloom and ready to be picked in September. Elderberries can be used in wine, syrup, jams, and jellies.

7. Wild mushrooms (different kinds): September is a great month for mushroom hunting because it marks the beginning of the season for many species. In September, it's common to find chanterelles, boletes, and hen of the woods wild mushroom species. From soups and stews to sauces and omelets, wild mushrooms can be utilized in a variety of recipes. Foraging for wild mushrooms requires caution, though, as some species can be dangerous.

8. Nettles (Urtica spp.): Nettles are a common wild herb around the globe. Nettle plant leaves can be picked in September and used as flavoring for meats, drinks, and soups. Iron, calcium, and other minerals are abundant in nettles.

In conclusion, September is a great month for foraging since a variety of wild plants and fruits are in season and ready to be picked. A fresh supply of nourishing and tasty wild plants can be enjoyed if you know what to search for and where to get it. To be safe, you should only harvest plants that you can clearly identify. Get outside to appreciate the delights of September foraging by strolling around the fields and woodlands.

CHAPTER TEN

OCTOBER
*

Foraging for wild plants is best done in October when many species are at their most flavorful and ripe. Some of the top wild plants to harvest in October are listed below:

1. Acorns are the nuts of oak trees and are a staple diet for many indigenous civilizations (Quercus spp.). Oak trees drop their acorns in October, making them accessible for foraging. Acorns can be used as a coffee substitute or crushed into flour for baking. Additionally, they include a lot of protein, fiber, and good fats.

2. Cranberries (Vaccinium spp.) are a tasty and tart wild fruit found in bogs and marshes all over the world. They include lots of antioxidants and vitamin C. Cranberries are ready for harvesting in October and can be added to sauces, and preserves, or used as a garnish for savory foods.

3. Wild grapes (Vitis spp.): In October, wild grapes are ready for picking and can be used to produce wine, jelly, or snacks. Wild grapes are a sweet and juicy wild fruit that can grow on vines in many places of the world.

4. Jerusalem artichoke (Helianthus tuberosus): This root vegetable is indigenous to North America and is also referred to as a sunchoke. Potassium, iron, and other minerals are abundant in them. Jerusalem artichokes are at their most flavorful in October and can be grilled as a side dish, or added to soups, or stews.

5. Diospyros spp. persimmons are a sweet and tasty wild fruit that are grown throughout most of the world. They include a lot of antioxidants, vitamin C, and A. Persimmons are ready to be picked around October and can be eaten raw or added to baked products.

6. Pecans (Carya illinoinensis) are a nut that is indigenous to North America and can be found growing on trees all over the world. They include lots of protein, good fats, and other nutrients. Pecans are ready to be picked around October and can be utilized in baking or as a snack.

7. Wild mushrooms (different kinds): October is a great month for collecting wild mushrooms because several species are at their growth peaks then. Shiitake, maitake, and oyster mushrooms are a few of the more well-liked wild mushroom species that can be discovered around October. From soups and stews to sauces and omelets, wild mushrooms can be utilized in a variety of recipes. Foraging for wild mushrooms requires caution, though, as some species can be dangerous.

8. Rosehips (Rosa spp.): Rosehips are a fruit that grows on wild rose plants and is distributed around the world. Rosehips are rich in antioxidants and vitamin C. Rosehips are ready to be picked around October and can be used to make tea, syrup, or jelly.

9. Burdock (Arctium spp.) is a common wild root vegetable around the globe. Burdock roots can be gathered in October and cooked as a side dish, soup, or stew. High fiber, potassium, and other nutritional levels are found in burdock root.

In conclusion, October is a great month for foraging because a variety of wild plants and fruits are in season and ready to be picked. A fresh supply of nourishing and tasty wild plants can be enjoyed if you know what to search for and where to get it.

CHAPTER ELEVEN
NOVEMBER
*

The harvest season ends in November, but there are still plenty of wild plants to forage for. Some of the greatest wild plants to harvest in November are listed below:

1. Rosehips (Rosa spp.): Rosehips are a fruit that grows on wild rose plants and is distributed around the world. Rosehips are rich in antioxidants and vitamin C. Rosehips can still be harvested in November and used to produce tea, syrup, or jelly.

2. Wild berries (different species): In many places of the world, wild berries are a delectable and nourishing wild meal. They include lots of antioxidants and vitamin C. Chokeberries, elderberries, and hawthorn berries are a few of the species that are still accessible for foraging in November. Jams, pies, or snacks can all be made using these berries.

3. Various varieties of nuts can be harvested in November, including hazelnuts, black walnuts, and chestnuts. These nuts are a good source of protein, fiber, and other nutrients. They can be added to salads, used in baking, or simply eaten as a snack.

4. Gaultheria procumbens, sometimes known as wintergreen, is a low-growing evergreen shrub that is indigenous to North America. Wintergreen leaves have a minty smell and are a natural source of methyl salicylate, which helps with pain. In November, wintergreen leaves can be collected and used to flavor dishes or brew tea.

5. Wild carrots (Daucus carota) are a wild relative of cultivated carrots and are also referred to as Queen Anne's Lace. Fibre, vitamin A, and other nutrients are abundant in wild carrots. Wild carrot roots can be picked in November and added to stews and soups.

6. Burdock (Arctium spp.) is a common wild root vegetable around the globe. Burdock roots can be picked in November and roasted as a side dish or used in soups and stews. High fiber, potassium, and other nutritional levels are found in burdock root.

7. Chicory (Cichorium intybus) is a wild herb that grows in fields and by the sides of roadways. Chicory leaves are rich in vitamins A and C and have a mildly bitter flavor. Chicory leaves can be picked in November and cooked or used in salads.

8. Wild garlic (Allium spp.) is a wild relative of garlic that can grow in woodland places and is often referred to as ramps. The nutritional and antioxidant content of wild garlic is high. Wild garlic bulbs and leaves can be gathered in November and utilized in a variety of cuisines, including soups, stews, salads, and pesto.

9. Pine needles (Pinus spp.): Foraged in November, pine needles are a fantastic wild meal. They can be used to create a tea or added for a distinctive flavor to soups and stews. Pine needles contain a lot of vitamin C and are antibacterial.

In conclusion, even though November signifies the end of the harvest season, there are still plenty of wild plants and fruits available for foraging. If you know what to search for and where to seek it, you can always have access to a fresh supply of nourishing and delicious wild plants. Always exercise caution when foraging, and only consume plants that you can positively identify.

CHAPTER TWELVE

DECEMBER

The winter solstice occurs in December, and although it may seem difficult to forage, some plants can still be collected in the wild. Some of the greatest wild plants to harvest in December are listed below:

1. Gaultheria procumbens, sometimes known as wintergreen, is a low-growing evergreen shrub that grows in woodlands and forests. Wintergreen leaves have a minty smell and are a natural source of methyl salicylate, which helps with pain. Wintergreen berries and leaves can be used to flavor food and create tea, respectively.

2. Pines (Pinus spp.): Pine bark and needles can be gathered in December and used to make infused oils, syrup, or tea. Pine needles have a pleasant flavor and are rich in vitamin C. Pine bark can be used to treat a variety of illnesses since it possesses anti-inflammatory and antiviral effects.

3. The fruit of the wild rose (Rosa spp.) plant, known as wild rose hips, is available for harvesting in December. Rose hips can be used to make tea, syrup, or jelly and are rich in vitamin C and antioxidants. They taste sweet and tart just a bit.

4. Ilex verticillata, sometimes known as winterberry, is a deciduous shrub that bears vivid red berries in the winter. They taste sour and contain lots of antioxidants. The berries can be collected and used to produce syrup, jelly, or tea.

5. Cedar (Cedrus spp.): In December, you can gather the needles and bark of cedar trees to produce tea or infused oils. The flavor of the needles is slightly lemony and pleasant. Cedar can be used to treat respiratory problems since it possesses antifungal and antibacterial qualities.

6. Honeysuckle (Lonicera spp.): In December, honeysuckle berries can be collected and used to produce syrup or tea. They taste delicious and contain lots of antioxidants. The mildly flavored leaves of honeysuckle can also be used to make tea.

7. Wild herb known as chickweed (Stellaria media) grows in fields and gardens. It can be picked in December and cooked or used for salads and soups. Chickweed has a flavor that is slightly sweet and nutty and is rich in vitamins A and C.

8. Mistletoe, or Viscum album, is a parasitic plant that develops on tree branches. Mistletoe can be used to treat a variety of illnesses since it possesses anti-inflammatory and antibacterial effects. Mistletoe berries and leaves can be collected in December and used to make tea or infused oils.

9. Wild ginger (Asarum spp.) is a low-growing plant that can be found in forests and woodlands. Wild ginger is rich in antioxidants and has a pungent, earthy flavor. In December, wild ginger roots can be gathered and used to season cuisine.

In conclusion, even though December could appear like a difficult month for foraging, the winter environment still has a lot of wild plants and fruits. If you know what to search for and where to seek it, you can always have access to a fresh supply of nourishing and delicious wild plants. Always exercise caution when foraging, and only consume plants that you can positively identify.

BOOK 6: PRESERVING EDIBLE WILD PLANTS

CHAPTER ONE

STORING WILD FOODS
*

The process of preserving wild foods has been employed by people for thousands of years. Wild edibles can be preserved and kept for future use by "storing" them. Utilizing techniques for food preservation like drying, canning, freezing, fermenting, pickling, smoking, and salting are all part of it.

For a number of reasons, it's important to store wild foods. First of all, it enables us to continuously gain from foraging. Wild edibles are frequently only available for a brief time, thus preserving them gives us access to them even when they are not in season. This can assist us in keeping up a balanced diet and reducing our reliance on prepared foods.

Additionally, preserving wild foods might lessen food waste. Food obtained through foraging is frequently in abundance, and storage can keep it from rotting and going to waste. In the modern world, when food waste is a significant environmental problem, this is especially crucial.

Last but not least, preserving wild foods helps us stay connected to the environment and our ancestors. Since humans have been gathering and conserving food for thousands of years, we may draw on this extensive history and learn from our ancestors by preserving wild foods.

An overview of how to preserve wild foods

There are various ways to preserve wild foods, each with benefits and drawbacks. The following are some of the most popular techniques:

• **Drying**: Drying includes removing moisture from food to stop germs and fungi that can ruin it from growing. Fruits, vegetables, and herbs can all be preserved using this method.

• **Canning**: In order to kill germs or other microbes, food must be placed in a sealed jar and heated to a high temperature. Fruits, vegetables, and meats are particularly well-suited to canning for preservation.

• To slow the growth of germs and other microorganisms, food is frozen and placed in a freezer. Fruits, vegetables, and meats can be preserved most effectively by freezing.

• **Fermenting**: Fermenting is the process of allowing a food's carbohydrates to be broken down by helpful bacteria, which produce lactic acid and other substances that help preserve the food and improve its flavor. In order to preserve vegetables, fermentation is especially effective. Examples of this include kimchi and sauerkraut.

• Pickling includes soaking food in vinegar, salt, and spice brine solution. In particular, this technique works well for preserving fruits and vegetables.

• When you smoke food, smoke from burning wood or other materials is inhaled. The preservation of meats and seafood is particularly well suited to this technique.

• **Salting**: To keep food from spoiling and to remove moisture, salt is used to cover food. The preservation of meats and seafood is particularly well suited to this technique.

Drying

One of the earliest and most basic ways of food preservation is drying. It entails taking away moisture from the food, which slows the development of germs and mold and averts food spoiling. There are other ways to dry things, such as air drying, sun drying, oven drying, and utilizing a food dehydrator. After dehydrating the food, it can be kept in an airtight container like a jar or plastic bag.

Advantages of Drying

- Compared to fresh or canned goods, dried foods are more portable and take up less space, making them perfect for trekking or camping trips.

- Food preservation by drying uses less energy, making it a sustainable choice.

- Dried foods can be kept without refrigeration for an extended period of time, sometimes up to a year or more.

- Many nutritional benefits, such as vitamins, minerals, and fiber, are retained by dried foods.

Disadvantages of drying

- Drying can make some foods lose their flavor, color, and texture. To make sure they are safe to eat, some things, like meat and fish, need to be further prepared before drying.

- Drying calls for patience and close attention to detail because either over- or under-drying can result in mold growth or in food that is excessively tough or brittle.

A few examples of dried wild foods

The following wild foods can be dried:

- Berries: You may air-dry or oven-dry wild berries like blueberries, raspberries, and blackberries to produce pleasant and wholesome snacks.

- Herbs: You can dry wild herbs like mint, thyme, and sage and use them to flavor soups, stews, and other foods.

- Wild mushrooms: To retain their savory, umami flavor, air-dry or oven-dry wild mushrooms like chanterelles and morels.

- Nuts: A wonderful and protein-rich snack can be made from dried and roasted wild nuts including acorns, chestnuts, and hickory nuts.

- Seeds: You can air-dry or oven-dry wild seeds like sunflower and pumpkin seeds to add to salads or trail mix.

- Jerky: To prepare a high-protein snack, wild game like venison or bison can be thinly sliced and dried in a dehydrator or oven.

The best methods for preserving wild foods

- **Select the proper foods**: Not all foods can be dried. Avoid foods that are heavy in fat or moisture, like avocado or coconut, and opt instead for foods that are low in moisture, including fruits, herbs, and seeds.

- Prepare the food by cleaning and trimming it as necessary before drying. To make sure they are safe to eat, some items, like meat or fish, may need to undergo further preparation, like brining or blanching.

- **Decide on a drying technique**: There are a number of ways to dry food, including air drying, sun drying, oven drying, and utilizing a food dehydrator. Select the drying technique that is most effective for the food you are drying and the resources you have at hand.

- **Keep an eye on the drying process**: Throughout the drying process, check the food often to make sure it is drying evenly and not over- or under-drying. Depending on the food and the drying technique, the drying time will change.

- **How to store dehydrated food**: After it has been dried, place it in an airtight container such as a jar or plastic bag. To ensure the dried food stays fresh for as long as possible, store the container in a cold, dry, and dark location. To maintain track of the food's freshness, mark the container with the name of the food and the date it was dried.

- **Rehydrate the food**: Before eating, some dry items, such as fruits or vegetables, may benefit from being rehydrated. You can rehydrate food by boiling it for a short time or soaking it in water for a few minutes.

- **Use the food**: Dried foods can be used in a variety of recipes, including soups and stews, trail mix, and as a spice for other cuisines. Be inventive and try out various uses for your dried wild foods.

A quick and efficient way to preserve wild foods is to dry them. Wild foods including berries, herbs, mushrooms, nuts, seeds, and even game meat can be preserved with this method. You may maintain the nutritional value and flavor of wild foods for a long time by adhering to best practices for drying, which include selecting the right foods, preparing them properly, selecting the right drying method, monitoring the drying process, and properly storing the dried food.

Canning

A common technique for preserving wild edibles is canning. To prevent food from spoiling, it includes heating sealed jars of food to kill bacteria and other germs, then keeping the jars in a cool, dry location. Wild foods can be successfully canned and kept fresh for up to a year or longer. The advantages and disadvantages of canning, various canning techniques, examples of canned wild foods, and best practices for canning wild foods are all covered in this section.

Advantages and Disadvantages of Canning:

The ability to preserve the nutritional value and flavor of wild foods is one of the canning's key advantages. Since wild foods may be kept for a long time and are portable, canning can be a practical way to store them. Canning does have certain disadvantages, though. One is that it can take a lot of time and equipment, such as jars, lids, a canner, and a thermometer. Additionally, botulism, an uncommon but serious sickness brought on by a toxin produced by the Clostridium botulinum bacteria, can be contracted by eating inadequately canned food. To ensure the food is safe, it is crucial to adhere to the best canning techniques.

Types of canning

Pressure canning and water bath canning are the two forms of canning. High-acid items including fruits, tomatoes, and pickles are canned in water baths. It entails immersing the jars in boiling water for a predetermined period of time, creating a vacuum seal that preserves the food. Low-acid items including vegetables, meats, and shellfish are suitable for pressure canning. It entails heating the jars in a pressure canner to a temperature higher than that required for water bath canning in order to eliminate any bacteria or other germs that could lead to deterioration.

Examples of canned wild foods include:

Fruits, vegetables, and meats from the wild can all be canned. The following are some instances of canned wild foods:

Wild berries can be preserved in the form of jams, jellies, or preserves. Examples include blueberries, raspberries, and blackberries.

Wild Mushrooms: Chanterelles and morels are two examples of wild mushrooms that can be preserved.

Wild Game: Game meat can be preserved in jars, including venison and wild turkey.

Tips for Preserving Wild Foods:

Observing canning best practices is crucial to guarantee the safety of your canned wild foods. Here are a few pieces of advice:

• Pick the correct ingredients: For canning, select high-quality, fresh wild foods. Foods that are spoiled more quickly if they are overripe or damaged should be avoided.

• Prepare the food correctly: Before canning, clean and carefully prepare the food. Washing produce, eliminating excess fat from meat, and cleaning mushrooms are all examples of this.

• Use the proper canning technique: pressure can low-acid items like vegetables and meats and water bath can high-acid foods like fruits.

• Keep an eye on the canning process: Use a thermometer to keep an eye on the temperature. Observe the processing temperatures and times advised for the particular type of canned food.

• Properly store the jars: Keep the jars out of direct sunlight in a cool, dry location. Regularly check the jars for symptoms of deterioration like bulging or leaking lids.

To sum up, canning is a useful method for preserving wild foods. They can retain their flavor and nutritional content while being fresh for extended periods of time. To ensure the food is safe, it is crucial to adhere to the best canning techniques. This entails selecting high-quality, fresh wild items, properly processing them, picking the best canning technique, keeping an eye on the canning procedure, and storing the jars in the right way. You may savor the delightful flavor of wild foods all year long while remaining safe if you adhere to these recommended practices.

Freezing

By lowering the temperature of the food down below its freezing point, freezing is a method of food preservation that prevents the growth of germs that lead to food degradation. A home freezer, a commercial freezer, or a cryogenic freezer can all be used to freeze anything. The food might be blended, chopped into chunks, or frozen intact.

Advantages and Disadvantages of freezing

As a method of food preservation, freezing offers many advantages. It is a rather simple and practical approach to keeping food fresh for a long time. Foods that are frozen can simply be thawed or reheated and utilized in a variety of ways. In addition, freezing preserves the food's nutritional content, as opposed to other techniques of preservation that risk destroying vital vitamins and minerals.

Some foods, particularly fruits and vegetables, might lose some of their texture and flavor when they are frozen. Freezing, however, has significant disadvantages as well.

Ice crystals may form during the freezing process, causing the food to lose quality and suffer cell damage. The texture and flavor of frozen meals can also change due to freezer burn, which happens when the food becomes dehydrated and the surface dries up.

Examples of freeze-able wild foods

The best way to preserve wild foods, especially those that are abundant during particular seasons, is to freeze them. Foods harvested from the wild that can be frozen include:

Berries: A common wild food that can be frozen is berries. Given their rich vitamin and antioxidant content, freezing them can help keep these vital minerals intact.

Fish is a fantastic source of protein and good fats. If you catch fish in large quantities, freezing it can help maintain its quality.

Game meat - To increase the shelf life of game meat, such as deer or wild boar, it can be frozen. For hunters who want to save their harvest for later use, this is extremely helpful.

The flavor and texture of wild mushrooms, which are a delicacy, can be preserved by freezing them.

The best ways to freeze wild foods

It is crucial to adhere to a few best practices while freezing wild foods in order to maintain the food's safety and high standard. To freeze wild foods, follow these suggestions:

• Thoroughly wash the food before freezing it. This will assist in clearing the food of any dirt or trash.

• Cut the food into smaller pieces to aid in a quicker and more consistent freezing process.

• Use containers or freezer bags made especially for freezing food. These containers will keep the food fresh and help prevent freezer burn.

• Write the date and the food's contents on the container or bag. This will make it easier for you to keep track of what is in the freezer and how long it has been there.

• Maintain a steady freezer temperature of 0°F or lower. Changing temperatures can lead to the formation of ice crystals, which can harm the food.

• To guarantee that frozen wild foods are still of high quality, use them within six months.

The best way to preserve food, even wild foods, is to freeze it. While freezing has many advantages, there are some negatives as well, therefore it is crucial to adhere to recommended procedures to guarantee that the food is kept safe and of a high standard. You may preserve your wild foods for later use and enjoy their flavor and nutritional advantages throughout the year by using these tips.

Fermentation

Food preservation through fermentation is a practice that dates back thousands of years. Utilizing bacteria, yeast, and other microorganisms, this process turns the sugars and starches in food into alcohol or organic acids. Using bacteria, yeast, and other microbes to ferment food entails converting sugars and starches into alcohol or organic acids. The food's shelf life is increased by this procedure, which produces an acidic environment that prevents the growth of dangerous germs and fungi. Fermentation can be carried out using a variety of methods, such as controlled fermentation, which involves adding particular strains of bacteria to the food, or wild fermentation, where the microorganisms occur naturally. This essay will discuss the idea of fermentation as a food preservation technique, as well as its advantages and disadvantages, as well as examples of wild foods that can be fermented and the best techniques for doing so.

Fermentation's advantages and disadvantages

As a means of food preservation, fermentation provides a number of advantages. It is a conventional and natural method of food preservation that does not call for synthetic additives. Additionally, by boosting the food's availability of vitamins and minerals, fermentation improves the food's nutritional value. Additionally, unlike preserved foods, fermented foods have a distinct flavor and texture. But fermentation also has significant disadvantages. Controlling the fermentation process can be difficult since it needs particular parameters to be successful, such as the appropriate temperature and pH. Some fermented foods may not be appealing to everyone because they have a strong scent or an acquired flavor.

Wild foods that can be fermented

Wild foods, especially those that are abundant during particular seasons, are exceptionally well-preserved by fermentation. The following are some instances of wild foods that can be fermented:

Wild berries: Rich in antioxidants, wild berries can be fermented to make delectable jams and preserves.

Wild mushrooms - In a variety of recipes, wild mushrooms can be fermented to create tasty sauces or condiments.

Game meat - Game meat can be fermented to make jerky or sausages that can be kept for a long time.

Wild greens - Dandelion or nettle leaves can be fermented to make kraut or kimchi, which are sour, tasty foods.

recommended methods for fermenting wild foods

It is crucial to adhere to a few basic practices while fermenting wild foods in order to maintain the food's safety and high standard. The following advice is provided for fermenting wild foods:

• Begin with top-notch, fresh ingredients. By doing this, the meal will be at its best and will ferment properly.

• Before usage, clean and sanitize all equipment. This will ensure that the fermentation process is successful and help avoid the formation of dangerous bacteria.

• To make sure the food is fermented properly, use a recipe or other instructions. You may accomplish the desired flavor and texture using this.

• Regularly keep an eye on the fermenting process. Look for any symptoms of food decomposition, such as mold or an offensive odor.

• Keep the fermented food in a dry, cool environment. By doing so, the fermentation process will be slowed down and the food's shelf life will be increased.

• Consume fermented wild foods as soon as possible. Fermented foods can be stored for a long time, but it's important to use them quickly to maintain quality.

Fermentation is an effective method of preserving food, including wild foods. While fermentation has several benefits, it also has some drawbacks, and it is essential to follow best practices to ensure that fermented food remains safe and of high quality. Fermenting is a natural and traditional way of preserving food that enhances its nutritional value, flavor, and texture. Fermented wild foods offer a unique taste of the local environment and season, making them a great way to connect with nature and local food sources. By following best practices for fermenting wild foods, we can ensure that we have a safe and healthy supply of preserved food that is both delicious and nutritious.

Other Methods of Preserving Wild Foods

Wild foods must be stored properly to increase their shelf life, maintain their nutritional value, and serve as a source of food during times of scarcity. Other techniques for preserving wild foods include pickling, smoking, and salting, in addition to freezing and fermenting. These approaches are still in use today and have been for centuries. Here, we'll look at pickling, smoking, and salting as ways to preserve wild foods, as well as their advantages and disadvantages and recommended applications.

Pickling: Food is preserved by pickling when it is submerged in vinegar or brine. The acidic environment produced by the vinegar or brine solution prevents the growth of dangerous germs and fungus, hence extending the food's shelf life. A variety of fruits, vegetables, and even meats can be pickled. As a way to preserve wild foods, pickling offers many advantages. It is a simple and affordable method of food preservation that requires little equipment and few ingredients. The food's flavor is also improved by pickling, which gives it a tangy, acidic flavor. Additionally, pickled foods are a healthful supplement to any diet because they are high in vitamins and minerals.

Pickling, however, also has significant disadvantages. It can take a while because the food needs to pickle properly for a few days or weeks. Some pickled foods could also be high in salt, making them unsuitable for anyone following a low-sodium diet. Finally, pickling can cause foods to lose some of their texture, turning softer or mushier.

Exposing food to smoke from burning wood chips or sawdust, smoking is a technique for preserving food. Natural preservatives included in the smoke produced by burning wood aid in preventing the development of dangerous bacteria and fungi. A variety of meats, fish, and cheeses can be smoked. As a way of preserving wild foods, smoking offers a number of advantages. It imparts a distinct smoky flavor and aroma to the meal that other techniques are unable to produce. Additionally improving the flavor of the food, smoking also makes it stiffer and chewier. Additionally, goods that have been smoked can be kept for a long time without refrigeration.

Smoking does, however, have significant disadvantages. The food may need to smoke properly for several hours or even days, which can take some time. Some smoked foods could also be high in sodium, making them unsuitable for anyone following a low-sodium diet. Last but not least, the price of equipment and wood chips may make smoking food more expensive than alternative ways of preserving wild foods.

Salting: By covering food with salt, we can preserve it. The environment is created by the salt's ability to pull moisture out of the food, which prevents the growth of dangerous germs and fungi. A variety of meats, fish, and even vegetables can be salted. As a way of preserving wild foods, salting has many advantages. It is a simple and affordable method of food preservation that only needs salt and minimal tools. By adding salt, food's flavor is improved and is given a savory, salty flavor. Salted food can also be kept for a long time without refrigeration.

Salting, however, also has certain disadvantages. It can take a long time because the food needs to be properly salted over the course of several days or weeks. Some salty foods could also be high in sodium, making them unsuitable for anyone following a low-sodium diet. Finally, during the salting process, meals may lose some of their texture and become softer or mushier.

Guidelines for using different techniques

No matter how wild foods are stored, there are a few basic practices to follow to guarantee their safety and good quality. These techniques include:

• **Make use of top-notch, fresh ingredients**: The quality of the finished product is directly impacted by the quality of the food that is being preserved. For the greatest outcomes, fresh, high-quality wild foods are required.

• **Carefully adhere to the directions**: Each technique for preserving wild foods comes with detailed instructions. The food will be safely and correctly preserved if these directions are strictly followed.

• **Use the right tools**: Whether storing food in a canning jar, a smoker, or a salt box, utilizing the right tools is crucial.

• **Keep the right temperatures**: Temperature control is crucial for safely keeping wild foods. Foods should be kept at the temperature specified for each storage technique.

Food that is stored in a cool, dry environment will survive longer and be less prone to spoil.

• **Date and label food**: To keep track of the age of stored wild foods and make sure they are used before going bad, it is crucial to date and label them.

• **Look for symptoms of decomposition**: Before eating wild food that has been stored, it's important to look for evidence of spoilage, such as mold, discoloration, or an unpleasant odor.

We can guarantee the quality and safety of our wild foods by adhering to these best practices.

Wild food is traditionally preserved via pickling, smoking, and salting, which are still practiced today. Each technique has advantages and disadvantages, but they are all capable of successfully preserving food. We can make sure we have a steady supply of nutritious and delicious preserved food by adhering to optimal procedures for storing wild foods.

The inclusion of delicious and nourishing wild foods into any diet might be tough in some places. Knowing how to preserve wild food resources effectively is crucial for maximizing their use. Several techniques for preserving wild foods were covered in this chapter, including canning, drying, freezing, fermenting, pickling, smoking, and salting. The best way to use depends on the food being preserved as well as individual tastes. Each method has advantages and disadvantages.

It's important to keep in mind that effective preservation methods are essential for maintaining the quality and safety of stored wild foods. Inadequate food storage can lead to food spoiling, which in extreme circumstances can result in disease and even death. Additionally, it's crucial to keep in mind that some wild foods can become hazardous if improperly stored, therefore it's crucial to do your homework on each food before storing it.

Keeping wild foods in storage can be a wonderful experience that enables us to eat scrumptious, nutritious food all year long. We can make sure that our preserved wild foods remain secure, nourishing, and tasty by adhering to proper storage procedures and selecting the best approach for each food. We invite readers to investigate the approaches covered in this article and to play with their preservation methods. Anyone may master the art of preserving wild foods with a little effort and perseverance, and reap the rewards of a balanced and sustainable diet.

BOOK 7: EDIBLE WILD PLANTS RECIPES

INTRODUCTION

Edible wild plants have been an essential human diet for thousands of years. They provide a natural source of nutrition and offer a diverse range of flavors and textures that can enhance any dish.

However, it is essential to remember that not all plants found in the wild are safe for consumption. Some wild plants can be poisonous and potentially fatal.

Therefore, one must be 100% sure their harvest plants are edible.

CHAPTER ONE

MAIN DISHES
*

RECIPE #1: Wild Greens and Mushroom Risotto

Cooking Time: 45 minutes

Servings: 4

Ingredients:

- 1 cup arborio rice
- 3 cups vegetable broth
- 1/2 cup white wine
- 1 onion, diced
- 2 cloves garlic, minced
- 1 cup mixed wild greens (such as dandelion, nettle, or lambs quarters), chopped
- 1 cup wild mushrooms (such as morels or chanterelles), chopped
- 1/4 cup grated Parmesan cheese
- Salt and pepper, to taste
- 2 tbsp olive oil

Instructions:

- In a large saucepan, heat olive oil over medium heat. Add onion and garlic and cook until softened.
- Add the rice to the saucepan and stir to coat with the oil. Cook for 2-3 minutes until the rice is toasted.
- Add the white wine to the saucepan and stir until absorbed.
- Add the vegetable broth, 1/2 cup at a time, constantly stirring until each addition is absorbed.
- After 15-20 minutes, add the wild greens and mushrooms to the saucepan and continue cooking until the rice is al dente.
- Remove from heat and stir in the Parmesan cheese. Season with salt and pepper to taste.
- Serve hot.

Nutritional Facts: Calories: 340, Carbs: 53g, Protein: 7g, Fat: 9g, Vitamin A: 15% DV, Vitamin C: 10% DV, Calcium: 10% DV, Iron: 20% DV

RECIPE #2: Stinging Nettle and Potato Soup

Cooking Time: 30 minutes

Servings: 6

Ingredients:

- 4 cups stinging nettle leaves, washed and chopped
- 2 large potatoes, peeled and chopped
- 1 onion, chopped
- 3 cloves garlic, minced
- 4 cups vegetable broth
- 1 cup milk
- Salt and pepper, to taste
- 2 tbsp olive oil

Instructions:

- In a large pot, heat olive oil over medium heat. Add onion and garlic and cook until softened.
- Add potatoes to the pot and stir to coat with the oil. Cook for 2-3 minutes until slightly softened.
- Add stinging nettle leaves and vegetable broth to the pot. Bring to a boil, then reduce heat and let simmer for 15-20 minutes.
- Using an immersion blender, blend the soup until smooth.
- Stir in the milk and season with salt and pepper to taste.
- Serve hot.

Nutritional Facts: Calories: 160, Carbs: 23g, Protein: 4g, Fat: 6g, Vitamin A: 130% DV, Vitamin C: 30% DV, Calcium: 15% DV, Iron: 20% DV.

RECIPE #3: Fiddlehead and Goat Cheese Omelette

Cooking Time: 20 minutes

Servings: 2

Ingredients:

- 4 eggs
- 1/2 cup fiddleheads, cleaned and chopped
- 1/4 cup crumbled goat cheese
- 1 tbsp butter
- Salt and pepper, to taste

Instructions:

- In a bowl, beat the eggs with salt and pepper.
- In a nonstick skillet, melt butter over medium heat. Add fiddleheads to the skillet and cook for 5-7 minutes until tender.
- Pour the beaten eggs into the skillet and cook for 2-3 minutes until the edges start to set.
- Sprinkle the goat cheese over half of the omelet and fold the other half over the cheese.
- Continue cooking until the cheese is melted and the eggs are set.
- Serve hot.

Nutritional Facts: Calories: 290, Carbs: 2g, Protein: 20g, Fat: 22g, Vitamin A: 20% DV, Vitamin C: 8% DV, Calcium: 10% DV, Iron: 15% DV

RECIPE #4: Wild Garlic and Potato Frittata

Cooking Time: 25 minutes

Servings: 4

Ingredients:

- 6 eggs
- 2 cups potatoes, peeled and chopped
- 1 cup wild garlic leaves, washed and chopped
- 1/4 cup grated Parmesan cheese
- Salt and pepper, to taste
- 2 tbsp olive oil

Instructions:

- In a bowl, beat the eggs with salt and pepper. Stir in the Parmesan cheese.
- In a nonstick skillet, heat olive oil over medium heat. Add potatoes to the skillet and cook for 5-7 minutes until slightly softened.
- Add the wild garlic leaves to the skillet and cook for 2-3 minutes until wilted.

- Pour the beaten egg mixture into the skillet, making sure the potatoes and garlic are evenly distributed.
- Cook for 5-7 minutes until the bottom is set.
- Place the skillet under the broiler and cook for 3-5 minutes until the top is golden brown.
- Serve hot.

Nutritional Facts: Calories: 320, Carbs: 18g, Protein: 17g, Fat: 20g, Vitamin A: 45% DV, Vitamin C: 25% DV, Calcium: 20% DV, Iron: 15% DV

RECIPE #5: Wild Mushroom and Thyme Pasta

Cooking Time: 30 minutes

Servings: 4

Ingredients:

- 12 oz pasta
- 1 lb mixed wild mushrooms (such as shiitake, oyster, and cremini), sliced
- 2 cloves garlic, minced
- 2 tbsp fresh thyme leaves
- 1/4 cup grated Parmesan cheese
- Salt and pepper, to taste
- 2 tbsp olive oil

Instructions:

- Cook pasta according to package instructions. Drain and set aside.
- In a large skillet, heat olive oil over medium heat. Add garlic and thyme to the skillet and cook for 1-2 minutes until fragrant.
- Add the mushrooms to the skillet and cook for 5-7 minutes until tender and slightly browned.
- Add the cooked pasta to the skillet and toss to coat with the mushroom mixture.
- Sprinkle Parmesan cheese over the pasta and season with salt and pepper to taste.
- Serve hot.

Nutritional Facts: Calories: 420, Carbs: 55g, Protein: 16g, Fat: 15g, Vitamin A: 10% DV, Vitamin C: 4% DV, Calcium: 20% DV, Iron: 25% DV

RECIPE #6: Dandelion Greens and Bacon Quiche

Cooking Time: 1 hour

Servings: 6

Ingredients:

- 1 pre-made pie crust
- 4 eggs
- 1 cup heavy cream
- 1/2 cup grated Parmesan cheese
- 4 slices bacon, cooked and crumbled
- 2 cups dandelion greens, washed and chopped
- Salt and pepper, to taste

Instructions:

- Preheat the oven to 375°F.
- Place the pre-made pie crust into a 9-inch pie dish.
- Whisk together eggs, heavy cream, Parmesan cheese, salt, and pepper in a bowl.
- Add dandelion greens and crumbled bacon to the mixture and stir to combine.
- Pour the mixture into the pie crust.
- Bake for 45-50 minutes until the center is set and the crust is golden brown.
- Let it cool for 10 minutes before serving.

Nutritional Facts: Calories: 460, Carbs: 20g, Protein: 13g, Fat: 37g, Vitamin A: 100% DV, Vitamin C: 20% DV, Calcium: 20% DV, Iron: 15% DV

RECIPE #7: Nettle and Potato Soup

Cooking Time: 45 minutes

Servings: 4

Ingredients:

- 4 cups nettle leaves, washed and chopped
- 2 cups potatoes, peeled and diced
- 1 onion, chopped
- 3 cloves garlic, minced
- 4 cups vegetable broth
- 2 tbsp olive oil
- Salt and pepper, to taste

Instructions:

- In a large pot, heat olive oil over medium heat. Add onion and garlic and cook until fragrant.
- Add diced potatoes and cook for 5 minutes until slightly softened.

- Add chopped nettle leaves to the pot and cook for 2-3 minutes until wilted.
- Pour vegetable broth over the mixture and bring it to a boil.
- Reduce heat and let the soup simmer for 30-35 minutes until the potatoes are fully cooked.
- Use an immersion blender to blend the soup until smooth.
- Season with salt and pepper to taste.
- Serve hot.

Nutritional Facts: Calories: 180, Carbs: 30g, Protein: 6g, Fat: 6g, Vitamin A: 200% DV, Vitamin C: 60% DV, Calcium: 10% DV, Iron: 25% DV.

RECIPE #8: Wild Onion and Mushroom Risotto

Cooking Time: 30 minutes

Servings: 4

Ingredients:

- 1 cup arborio rice
- 1/2 cup white wine
- 4 cups vegetable broth
- 1 onion, chopped
- 2 cups wild mushrooms, sliced
- 1/4 cup grated Parmesan cheese
- 2 tbsp butter
- Salt and pepper, to taste

Instructions:

- In a large pot, heat vegetable broth and keep it simmering on low heat.
- In a separate pot, melt butter over medium heat. Add chopped onion and cook until translucent.
- Add sliced wild mushrooms to the pot and cook for 5-7 minutes until tender.
- Add arborio rice to the pot and stir to coat with the butter mixture.
- Pour white wine into the pot and stir until absorbed.
- Begin adding the simmering vegetable broth, one ladle at a time.
- Stir the rice constantly until each ladleful of broth is fully absorbed before adding the next one.
- Continue adding broth and stirring until the rice is cooked al dente.
- Stir in grated Parmesan cheese and chopped wild onions.
- Season with salt and pepper to taste.
- Serve hot.

Nutritional Facts: Calories: 360, Carbs: 50g, Protein: 9g, Fat: 10g, Vitamin A: 6% DV, Vitamin C: 2% DV, Calcium: 10% DV, Iron: 20% DV

RECIPE #9: Chanterelle and Herb Frittata

Cooking Time: 25 minutes

Servings: 4

Ingredients:

- 8 eggs
- 1/4 cup heavy cream
- 1 cup chanterelle mushrooms, cleaned and chopped
- 1/4 cup chopped fresh herbs (such as parsley, thyme, and chives)
- 2 tbsp butter
- Salt and pepper, to taste

Instructions:

- Preheat the oven to 375°F.
- Whisk together eggs, heavy cream, salt, and pepper in a large bowl.
- In an oven-safe skillet, melt butter over medium heat. Add chopped chanterelle mushrooms and sauté for 5-7 minutes until golden brown.
- Pour the egg mixture into the skillet and stir to combine.
- Sprinkle chopped fresh herbs over the mixture.
- Let the frittata cook for 5-7 minutes until the edges start to set.
- Transfer the skillet to the oven and bake for 10-15 minutes until the center is fully set.
- Let it cool for a few minutes before slicing and serving.

Nutritional Facts: Calories: 280, Carbs: 3g, Protein: 19g, Fat: 21g, Vitamin A: 30% DV, Vitamin C: 4% DV, Calcium: 10% DV, Iron: 15% DV.

RECIPE #10: Wild Greens and Mushroom Lasagna

Cooking Time: 1 hour and 15 minutes

Servings: 8

Ingredients:

- 12 lasagna noodles, cooked
- 4 cups mixed wild greens (such as nettles, dandelion greens, and sorrel), washed and chopped
- 3 cups mushrooms, sliced
- 4 cups tomato sauce
- 2 cups ricotta cheese
- 1 cup grated Parmesan cheese
- 2 tbsp olive oil

Instructions:

- Preheat the oven to 375°F.
- In a large pot, heat olive oil over medium heat. Add sliced mushrooms and cook for 5-7 minutes until tender.
- Add chopped mixed wild greens to the pot and cook for 2-3 minutes until wilted.
- Mix ricotta cheese, grated Parmesan cheese, salt, and pepper separately.
- In a 9x13-inch baking dish, spread a layer of tomato sauce on the bottom.
- Arrange four cooked lasagna noodles on top of the tomato sauce.
- Spread a layer of the ricotta mixture on top of the noodles.
- Add a layer of the mushroom and wild greens mixture.
- Repeat layers of noodles, ricotta mixture, mushrooms, and wild greens until all ingredients are used.
- Finish with a layer of tomato sauce on top.
- Cover the baking dish with foil and bake for 45 minutes.
- Remove the foil and bake for 10-15 minutes until the top is golden brown and bubbly.
- Let it cool for a few minutes before slicing and serving.

Nutritional Facts: Calories: 470, Carbs: 43g, Protein: 24g, Fat: 22g, Vitamin A: 80% DV, Vitamin C: 30% DV, Calcium: 50% DV, Iron: 20% DV.

Try these ten edible wild plants' main dishes recipes at home. Additionally, nutritional facts may vary depending on the specific ingredients and brands used in the recipes.

CHAPTER TWO
SIDE DISHES
*

RECIPE #1: Wild Garlic and Potato Salad

Cooking Time: 30 minutes

Servings: 4

Ingredients:

- 1 lb potatoes, diced
- 1/2 cup wild garlic leaves, chopped
- 1/4 cup mayonnaise
- 1/4 cup plain Greek yogurt
- 2 tbsp Dijon mustard
- 2 tbsp apple cider vinegar
- Salt and pepper, to taste

Instructions:

- In a large pot, boil diced potatoes until tender.
- Drain the potatoes and let them cool for a few minutes.
- Mix chopped wild garlic leaves, mayonnaise, Greek yogurt, Dijon mustard, apple cider vinegar, salt, and pepper in a separate bowl.
- Add the dressing to the potatoes and stir to combine.
- Serve the potato salad at room temperature or chilled.

Nutritional Facts: Calories: 210, Carbs: 26g, Protein: 5g, Fat: 10g, Vitamin A: 10% DV, Vitamin C: 25% DV, Calcium: 6% DV, Iron: 10% DV

RECIPE #2: Fiddlehead Ferns with Lemon and Garlic

Cooking Time: 15 minutes

Servings: 4

Ingredients:

- 1 lb fiddlehead ferns, washed and trimmed
- 2 tbsp butter
- 2 cloves garlic, minced
- 1 tbsp lemon juice
- Salt and pepper, to taste

Instructions:

- In a large pot, boil fiddlehead ferns for 10-12 minutes until tender.
- Drain the ferns and let them cool for a few minutes.
- In a skillet, melt butter over medium heat. Add minced garlic and sauté for 1-2 minutes until fragrant.
- Add the boiled fiddlehead ferns to the skillet and toss to coat in the garlic butter.
- Drizzle with lemon juice and season with salt and pepper to taste.
- Serve hot.

Nutritional Facts: Calories: 70, Carbs: 5g, Protein: 3g, Fat: 5g, Vitamin A: 25% DV, Vitamin C: 20% DV, Calcium: 6% DV, Iron: 15% DV

RECIPE #3: Wild Mushroom and Quinoa Pilaf

Cooking Time: 30 minutes

Servings: 4

Ingredients:

- 1 cup quinoa, rinsed and drained
- 2 cups chicken or vegetable broth
- 2 cups mixed wild mushrooms, cleaned and sliced
- 1 onion, chopped
- 2 cloves garlic, minced
- 2 tbsp olive oil
- Salt and pepper, to taste

Instructions:

- In a large pot, bring chicken or vegetable broth to a boil. Add rinsed quinoa and stir.
- Cover the pot and simmer for 15-20 minutes until the quinoa is tender and the broth has been absorbed.
- In a skillet, heat olive oil over medium heat. Add chopped onion and minced garlic, and sauté for 2-3 minutes until soft.
- Add sliced wild mushrooms to the skillet and sauté for 5-7 minutes until tender.
- Mix the cooked quinoa and sautéed mushroom mixture in a serving dish.
- Season with salt and pepper to taste.
- Serve hot.

Nutritional Facts: Calories: 290, Carbs: 39g, Protein: 10g, Fat: 11g, Vitamin A: 0% DV, Vitamin C: 6% DV, Calcium: 4% DV, Iron: 15% DV

RECIPE #4: Dandelion Greens Salad

Cooking Time: 15 minutes

Servings: 4

Ingredients:

- 4 cups dandelion greens, washed and chopped
- 1/4 cup red onion, sliced
- 1/4 cup toasted walnuts, chopped
- 1/4 cup crumbled feta cheese
- 2 tbsp balsamic vinegar
- 2 tbsp olive oil
- 1 tsp honey
- Salt and pepper, to taste

Instructions:

- Add chopped dandelion greens, sliced red onion, and chopped walnuts in a large mixing bowl.
- Mix balsamic vinegar, olive oil, honey, salt, and pepper in a separate bowl.
- Pour the dressing over the salad mixture and toss to combine.
- Top with crumbled feta cheese.
- Serve chilled.

Nutritional Facts: Calories: 140, Carbs: 8g, Protein: 4g, Fat: 11g, Vitamin A: 160% DV, Vitamin C: 20% DV, Calcium: 15% DV, Iron: 15% DV.

RECIPE #5: Wild Berry Compote

Cooking Time: 20 minutes

Servings: 4

Ingredients:

- 2 cups mixed wild berries (such as blackberries, blueberries, and raspberries)
- 1/4 cup honey
- 2 tbsp lemon juice
- 1 tsp cornstarch

Instructions:

- Combine mixed wild berries, honey, and lemon juice in a medium saucepan.

- Bring to a boil over medium heat, stirring occasionally.
- Reduce heat and let the mixture simmer for 10-12 minutes until the berries have broken down and released their juices.
- In a small bowl, mix cornstarch and 1 tbsp of water.
- Add the cornstarch mixture to the berry mixture and stir to combine.
- Cook for an additional 2-3 minutes until the compote has thickened.
- Remove from heat and let it cool for a few minutes before serving.
- Serve the wild berry compote warm or chilled as a side to yogurt, ice cream, or pancakes.

Nutritional Facts: Calories: 80, Carbs: 21g, Protein: 1g, Fat: 0g, Vitamin A: 4% DV, Vitamin C: 25% DV, Calcium: 2% DV, Iron: 4% DV.

RECIPE #6: Garlic Mustard Pesto

Cooking Time: 15 minutes

Servings: 8

Ingredients:

- 2 cups garlic mustard leaves, washed and dried
- 1/2 cup walnuts
- 1/2 cup grated Parmesan cheese
- 1/4 cup olive oil
- 2 tbsp lemon juice
- Salt and pepper, to taste

Instructions:

- In a food processor, pulse garlic mustard leaves, walnuts, and Parmesan cheese until well combined.
- Slowly add olive oil and lemon juice while pulsing the mixture.
- Add salt and pepper to taste.
- Serve the garlic mustard pesto as a dip, spread, or sauce for vegetables, bread, or pasta.

Nutritional Facts: Calories: 180, Carbs: 3g, Protein: 5g, Fat: 17g, Vitamin A: 45% DV, Vitamin C: 10% DV, Calcium: 15% DV, Iron: 10% DV.

RECIPE #7: Wild Mushroom Saute

Cooking Time: 20 minutes

Servings: 4

Ingredients:

- 4 cups wild mushrooms (such as morels, chanterelles, or oyster mushrooms), cleaned and sliced
- 2 cloves garlic, minced
- 2 tbsp butter
- 1/4 cup fresh parsley, chopped
- Salt and pepper, to taste

Instructions:

- In a large skillet, melt butter over medium heat.
- Add sliced mushrooms and minced garlic to the skillet and saute until the mushrooms are soft and lightly browned about 10-12 minutes.
- Add salt and pepper to taste.
- Sprinkle chopped parsley over the mushrooms before serving.
- Serve the wild mushroom saute as a side dish or over toast.

Nutritional Facts: Calories: 80, Carbs: 4g, Protein: 4g, Fat: 7g, Vitamin A: 10% DV, Vitamin C: 2% DV, Calcium: 2% DV, Iron: 6% DV

RECIPE #8: Nettle Soup

Cooking Time: 30 minutes

Servings: 4

Ingredients:

- 4 cups fresh nettle leaves, washed and dried
- 1 onion, chopped
- 2 cloves garlic, minced
- 4 cups vegetable broth
- 1/4 cup heavy cream
- Salt and pepper, to taste

Instructions:

- In a large pot, saute chopped onion and minced garlic until the onion is soft and translucent, about 5-7 minutes.
- Add nettle leaves to the pot and saute until wilted about 3-5 minutes.

- Add vegetable broth to the pot and bring to a boil.
- Reduce heat and let the soup simmer for 15-20 minutes.
- Using an immersion blender, puree the soup until smooth.
- Stir in heavy cream and salt and pepper to taste.
- Serve the nettle soup hot as a side dish or appetizer.

Nutritional Facts: Calories: 90, Carbs: 10g, Protein: 4g, Fat: 4g, Vitamin A: 200% DV, Vitamin C: 10% DV, Calcium: 20% DV, Iron: 10% DV

RECIPE #9: Wild Greens Frittata

Cooking Time: 30 minutes

Servings: 4

Ingredients:

- 2 cups mixed wild greens (such as dandelion, chickweed, and lambs quarters), washed and chopped
- 6 eggs
- 1/4 cup milk
- 1/2 cup grated Parmesan cheese
- 2 tbsp olive oil
- Salt and pepper, to taste

Instructions:

- Preheat oven to 350°F (175°C).
- In a large bowl, beat eggs with milk and grated Parmesan cheese.
- Add chopped wild greens to the bowl and mix well.
- Heat olive oil in a 10-inch oven-safe skillet over medium heat.
- Pour the egg and greens mixture into the skillet and cook for 5-7 minutes or until the edges start to set.
- Transfer the skillet to the preheated oven and bake for another 10-12 minutes, until the frittata is set and lightly golden on top.
- Season with salt and pepper to taste.
- Serve the wild greens frittata hot or cold as a side dish or light meal.

Nutritional Facts: Calories: 220, Carbs: 5g, Protein: 16g, Fat: 15g, Vitamin A: 70% DV, Vitamin C: 20% DV, Calcium: 25% DV, Iron: 15% DV

RECIPE #10: Spicy Cattail Shoots

Cooking Time: 15 minutes

Servings: 4

Ingredients:

- 2 cups cattail shoots, cleaned and sliced
- 2 cloves garlic, minced
- 2 tbsp soy sauce
- 1 tbsp honey
- 1 tbsp sesame oil
- 1 tsp red pepper flakes
- Salt and pepper, to taste

Instructions:

- Whisk together soy sauce, honey, sesame oil, and red pepper flakes in a small bowl.
- Heat a large skillet over medium heat.
- Add sliced cattail shoots and minced garlic to the skillet and saute for 5-7 minutes or until the shoots are tender.
- Pour the soy sauce mixture over the cattail shoots and stir well.
- Cook for another 1-2 minutes until the sauce has thickened and coated the shoots.
- Season with salt and pepper to taste.
- Serve the spicy cattail shoots as a side dish or appetizer.

Nutritional Facts: Calories: 70, Carbs: 10g, Protein: 3g, Fat: 3g, Vitamin A: 40% DV, Vitamin C: 15% DV, Calcium: 2% DV, Iron: 6% DV.

CHAPTER THREE

SOUP DISHES
*

RECIPE #1: Wild Nettle Soup

Cooking Time: 30 minutes

Servings: 6

Ingredients:

- 4 cups fresh nettle leaves, washed and chopped
- 1 onion, chopped
- 2 garlic cloves, minced
- 4 cups vegetable broth
- 1/2 cup heavy cream
- 2 tbsp olive oil
- Salt and pepper, to taste

Instructions:

- In a large pot, heat olive oil over medium heat.
- Add chopped onion and minced garlic to the pot and saute for 3-4 minutes or until the onion is translucent.
- Add chopped nettle leaves to the pot and saute for another 2-3 minutes or until they have wilted.
- Pour vegetable broth into the pot and bring to a boil.
- Reduce heat to low and let simmer for 15-20 minutes or until the nettle leaves are tender.
- Remove from heat and let cool slightly.

- Using an immersion blender, puree the soup until smooth.
- Stir in heavy cream and season with salt and pepper to taste.
- Serve the nettle soup hot.

Nutritional Facts: Calories: 120, Carbs: 8g, Protein: 3g, Fat: 9g, Vitamin A: 80% DV, Vitamin C: 30% DV, Calcium: 10% DV, Iron: 15% DV.

RECIPE #2: Wild Mushroom Soup

Cooking Time: 45 minutes

Servings: 4

Ingredients:

- 2 cups wild mushrooms, cleaned and chopped
- 1 onion, chopped
- 2 garlic cloves, minced
- 4 cups vegetable broth
- 1/2 cup heavy cream
- 2 tbsp butter
- Salt and pepper, to taste

Instructions:

- In a large pot, melt butter over medium heat.
- Add chopped onion and minced garlic to the pot and saute for 3-4 minutes or until the onion is translucent.
- Add chopped mushrooms to the pot and saute for another 5-7 minutes or until tender.
- Pour vegetable broth into the pot and bring to a boil.
- Reduce heat to low and let simmer for 20-25 minutes or until the mushrooms are fully cooked.
- Remove from heat and let cool slightly.
- Using an immersion blender, puree the soup until smooth.
- Stir in heavy cream and season with salt and pepper to taste.
- Serve the mushroom soup hot.

Nutritional Facts: Calories: 160, Carbs: 7g, Protein: 3g, Fat: 14g, Vitamin A: 10% DV, Vitamin C: 8% DV, Calcium: 2% DV, Iron: 6% DV

RECIPE #3: Wild Leek and Potato Soup

Cooking Time: 35 minutes

Servings: 6

Ingredients:

- 2 cups wild leeks, cleaned and chopped
- 4 potatoes, peeled and diced
- 1 onion, chopped
- 4 cups vegetable broth
- 1/2 cup heavy cream
- 2 tbsp olive oil
- Salt and pepper, to taste

Instructions:

- In a large pot, heat olive oil over medium heat.
- Add chopped onion to the pot and saute for 3-4 minutes or until the onion is translucent.
- Add diced potatoes to the pot and saute for 5-7 minutes or until they soften.
- Add chopped wild leeks to the pot and saute for another 2-3 minutes or until they have wilted.
- Pour vegetable broth into the pot and bring to a boil.
- Reduce heat to low and let simmer for 20-25 minutes until the potatoes are fully cooked.
- Remove from heat and let cool slightly.

- Using an immersion blender, puree the soup until smooth.
- Stir in heavy cream and season with salt and pepper to taste.
- Serve the wild leek and potato soup hot.

Nutritional Facts: Calories: 180, Carbs: 22g, Protein: 4g, Fat: 9g, Vitamin A: 60% DV, Vitamin C: 45% DV, Calcium: 6% DV, Iron: 10% DV

RECIPE #4: Wild Garlic Soup

Cooking Time: 25 minutes

Servings: 4

Ingredients:

- 2 cups wild garlic leaves, washed and chopped
- 1 onion, chopped
- 2 garlic cloves, minced
- 4 cups vegetable broth
- 1/2 cup heavy cream
- 2 tbsp butter
- Salt and pepper, to taste

Instructions:

- In a large pot, melt butter over medium heat.
- Add chopped onion and minced garlic to the pot and saute for 3-4 minutes or until the onion is translucent.
- Add chopped wild garlic leaves to the pot and saute for another 2-3 minutes or until they have wilted.
- Pour vegetable broth into the pot and bring to a boil.
- Reduce heat to low and simmer for 15-20 minutes until the garlic leaves are tender.
- Remove from heat and let cool slightly.
- Using an immersion blender, puree the soup until smooth.
- Stir in heavy cream and season with salt and pepper to taste.
- Serve the wild garlic soup hot.

Nutritional Facts: Calories: 120, Carbs: 8g, Protein: 3g, Fat: 9g, Vitamin A: 100% DV, Vitamin C: 20% DV, Calcium: 10% DV, Iron: 10% DV

RECIPE #5: Wild Asparagus Soup

Cooking Time: 40 minutes

Servings: 6

Ingredients:

- 2 cups wild asparagus, cleaned and chopped
- 1 onion, chopped
- 2 garlic cloves, minced
- 4 cups vegetable broth
- 1/2 cup heavy cream
- 2 tbsp olive oil
- Salt and pepper, to taste

Instructions:

- In a large pot, heat olive oil over medium heat.
- Add chopped onion and minced garlic to the pot and saute for 3-4 minutes or until the onion is translucent.
- Add chopped wild asparagus to the pot and saute for another 5-7 minutes or until tender.
- Pour vegetable broth into the pot and bring to a boil.
- Reduce heat to low and let simmer for 20-25 minutes until the asparagus is fully cooked.
- Remove from heat and let cool slightly.
- Using an immersion blender, puree the soup until smooth.
- Stir in heavy cream and season with salt and pepper to taste.
- Serve the wild asparagus soup hot.

Nutritional Facts: Calories: 150, Carbs: 9g, Protein: 3g, Fat: 12g, Vitamin A: 30% DV.

RECIPE #6: Nettle Soup

Cooking Time: 30 minutes

Servings: 4

Ingredients:

- 4 cups fresh nettle leaves, washed and chopped
- 1 onion, chopped
- 2 garlic cloves, minced
- 4 cups vegetable broth
- 1/2 cup heavy cream
- 2 tbsp olive oil
- Salt and pepper, to taste

Instructions:

- In a large pot, heat olive oil over medium heat.

- Add chopped onion and minced garlic to the pot and saute for 3-4 minutes or until the onion is translucent.
- Add chopped nettle leaves to the pot and saute for another 5-7 minutes or until they are wilted.
- Pour vegetable broth into the pot and bring to a boil.
- Reduce heat to low and let simmer for 15-20 minutes or until the nettles are tender.
- Remove from heat and let cool slightly.
- Using an immersion blender, puree the soup until smooth.
- Stir in heavy cream and season with salt and pepper to taste.
- Serve the nettle soup hot.

Nutritional Facts: Calories: 150, Carbs: 10g, Protein: 4g, Fat: 11g, Vitamin A: 70% DV, Vitamin C: 40% DV, Calcium: 20% DV, Iron: 20% DV

RECIPE #7: Wild Mushroom Soup

Cooking Time: 35 minutes

Servings: 6

Ingredients:

- 2 cups wild mushrooms, cleaned and sliced
- 1 onion, chopped
- 2 garlic cloves, minced
- 4 cups vegetable broth
- 1/2 cup heavy cream
- 2 tbsp butter
- Salt and pepper, to taste

Instructions:

- In a large pot, melt butter over medium heat.
- Add chopped onion and minced garlic to the pot and saute for 3-4 minutes or until the onion is translucent.
- Add sliced mushrooms to the pot and saute for another 5-7 minutes or until tender.
- Pour vegetable broth into the pot and bring to a boil.
- Reduce heat to low and let simmer for 15-20 minutes until the mushrooms are fully cooked.
- Remove from heat and let cool slightly.
- Using an immersion blender, puree the soup until smooth.
- Stir in heavy cream and season with salt and pepper to taste.
- Serve the wild mushroom soup hot.

Nutritional Facts: Calories: 130, Carbs: 7g, Protein: 3g, Fat: 10g, Vitamin A: 10% DV, Vitamin C: 6% DV, Calcium: 2% DV, Iron: 6% DV

RECIPE #8: Wild Rice and Nettle Soup

Cooking Time: 45 minutes

Servings: 6

Ingredients:

- 1 cup wild rice, rinsed and drained
- 4 cups vegetable broth
- 4 cups fresh nettle leaves, washed and chopped
- 1 onion, chopped
- 2 garlic cloves, minced
- 1/2 cup heavy cream
- 2 tbsp olive oil, salt and pepper, to taste

Instructions:

- In a large pot, heat olive oil over medium heat.
- Add chopped onion and minced garlic to the pot and saute for 3-4 minutes or until the onion is translucent.
- Add chopped nettle leaves to the pot and saute for another 5-7 minutes or until they are wilted.
- Pour vegetable broth into the pot and bring to a boil.
- Add rinsed and drained wild rice to the pot, reduce heat to low, and let simmer for 30-35 minutes or until the rice is tender.
- Add heavy cream to the pot and stir until well combined.
- Season with salt and pepper to taste.
- Serve the wild rice and nettle soup hot.

Nutritional Facts: Calories: 210, Carbs: 22g, Protein: 5g, Fat: 12g, Vitamin A: 70% DV, Vitamin C: 20% DV, Calcium: 8% DV, Iron: 15% DV.

RECIPE #9: Dandelion Greens and Potato Soup

Cooking Time: 40 minutes

Servings: 4

Ingredients:

- 4 cups dandelion greens, washed and chopped
- 2 potatoes, peeled and chopped
- 1 onion, chopped
- 2 garlic cloves, minced
- 4 cups vegetable broth

- 1/2 cup heavy cream
- 2 tbsp butter, salt and pepper, to taste

Instructions:

- In a large pot, melt butter over medium heat.
- Add chopped onion and minced garlic to the pot and saute for 3-4 minutes or until the onion is translucent.
- Add chopped potatoes to the pot and saute for 5-7 minutes or until tender.
- Pour vegetable broth into the pot and bring to a boil.
- Add chopped dandelion greens to the pot, reduce heat to low, and let simmer for 15-20 minutes until the greens are wilted, and the potatoes are fully cooked.
- Remove from heat and let cool slightly.
- Using an immersion blender, puree the soup until smooth.
- Stir in heavy cream and season with salt and pepper to taste.
- Serve the dandelion greens and hot potato soup.

Nutritional Facts: Calories: 190, Carbs: 18g, Protein: 4g, Fat: 12g, Vitamin A: 90% DV, Vitamin C: 30% DV, Calcium: 15% DV, Iron: 20% DV

RECIPE #10: Chickweed and Carrot Soup

Cooking Time: 30 minutes

Servings: 4

Ingredients:

- 4 cups chickweed, washed and chopped
- 2 carrots, peeled and chopped
- 1 onion, chopped
- 2 garlic cloves, minced
- 4 cups vegetable broth
- 1/2 cup heavy cream
- 2 tbsp olive oil, salt and pepper, to taste

Instructions:

- In a large pot, heat olive oil over medium heat.
- Add chopped onion and minced garlic to the pot and saute for 3-4 minutes or until the onion is translucent.
- Add chopped carrots to the pot and saute for another 5-7 minutes or until tender.
- Pour vegetable broth into the pot and bring to a boil.
- Add chopped chickweed to the pot, reduce heat to low, and let simmer for 10-15 minutes until the

chickweed is wilted and the carrots are fully cooked.
- Remove from heat and let cool slightly.
- Using an immersion blender, puree the soup until smooth.
- Stir in heavy cream and season with salt and pepper to taste
- Serve the chickweed and carrot soup hot.

Nutritional Facts: Calories: 190, Carbs: 16g, Protein: 4g, Fat: 12g, Vitamin A: 370% DV, Vitamin C: 35% DV, Calcium: 10% DV, Iron: 10% DV.

CHAPTER FOUR
DESERT AND SNACK RECIPES
*

RECIPE #1: Elderflower Fritters

Cooking Time: 20 minutes

Servings: 4

Ingredients:

- 1 cup elderflower blossoms
- 1 cup flour
- 1 egg
- 1/2 cup milk
- 1 tbsp sugar
- 1 tsp baking powder
- 1/4 tsp salt
- Oil for frying, Powdered sugar for topping

Instructions:

- Mix flour, sugar, baking powder, and salt in a bowl.
- In a separate bowl, whisk egg and milk together.
- Add the wet ingredients to the dry ingredients and mix until smooth.
- Dip the elderflower blossoms in the batter and fry in oil until golden brown.
- Serve hot with powdered sugar on top.

Nutritional Facts: Calories: 300, Carbs: 45g, Protein: 7g, Fat: 10g, Vitamin C: 10% of the daily value.

RECIPE #2: Wild Blueberry Bars

Cooking Time: 50 minutes

Servings: 12

Ingredients:

- 1 1/2 cups flour
- 1/2 cup rolled oats
- 1/2 cup brown sugar
- 1/2 cup butter, melted
- 1 tsp vanilla extract
- 1/4 tsp salt
- 2 cups wild blueberries
- 2 tbsp flour
- 1/4 cup sugar, 1 tbsp lemon juice

Instructions:

- Preheat the oven to 350°F (180°C).
- Mix flour, oats, brown sugar, melted butter, vanilla extract, and salt in a bowl.
- Press 2/3 of the mixture into a greased 9x9-inch (23x23 cm) baking pan.
- Mix blueberries, flour, sugar, and lemon juice separately.
- Spread the blueberry mixture over the crust.
- Sprinkle the remaining crust mixture over the blueberry layer.
- Bake for 35-40 minutes or until golden brown.
- Let cool before cutting into bars.

Nutritional Facts (per serving): Calories: 220, Carbs: 34g, Protein: 2g, Fat: 9g, Vitamin C: 6% of the daily value

RECIPE #3: Dandelion Root Coffee

Cooking Time: 20 minutes

Servings: 4

Ingredients:

- 4 cups of chopped dandelion roots
- Water
- Milk or cream (optional)
- Sweetener (optional)

Instructions:

- Preheat the oven to 350°F (180°C).
- Rinse the dandelion roots and chop them into small pieces.
- Spread the chopped roots on a baking sheet and roast in the oven for 15-20 minutes or until dark and fragrant.
- Boil 4 cups of water and add the roasted dandelion roots.
- Simmer for 10-15 minutes.
- Strain the liquid through a fine-mesh sieve or cheesecloth.
- Serve hot with milk or cream and sweetener if desired.

Nutritional Facts: Calories: 10, Carbs: 3g, Protein: 0g, Fat: 0g, Vitamin A: 60% of the daily value, Wild Rose Petal Jam, Cooking Time: 1 hour

RECIPE #4: Wild Rose Petal Jam

Cooking Time: 1 hour

Servings: 16

Ingredients:

- 2 cups of wild rose petals
- 2 cups of sugar
- 2 cups of water

Instructions:

- Rinse the rose petals and remove the white base from each petal.
- Mix the water and sugar in a pot and bring them to a boil.
- Add the rose petals and simmer for about 45-60 minutes, occasionally stirring until the mixture thickens.

- Remove from heat and let cool for 10-15 minutes.
- Pour the jam into sterilized jars and let cool completely before sealing.

Nutritional Facts: Calories: 120, Carbs: 31g, Protein: 0g, Fat: 0g, Vitamin C: 10% of the daily value

RECIPE #5: Maple and Nutmeg Roasted Acorn Squash Seeds

Cooking Time: 30 minutes

Servings: 4

Ingredients:

- 2 cups of acorn squash seeds
- 2 tbsp of maple syrup
- 1 tbsp of melted butter or oil
- 1/4 tsp of nutmeg
- Salt to taste

Instructions:

- Preheat the oven to 350°F (180°C).
- Rinse the acorn squash seeds and remove any flesh or strings.
- Pat dry with a paper towel and spread on a baking sheet.
- Mix the maple syrup, melted butter or oil, nutmeg, and salt in a bowl.
- Drizzle the mixture over the acorn squash seeds and toss to coat.
- Bake for 20-30 minutes, stirring occasionally, until the seeds are golden brown and crispy.
- Let cool before serving.

Nutritional Facts: Calories: 180, Carbs: 15g, Protein: 6g, Fat: 12g, Vitamin A: 20% of the daily value.

RECIPE #6: Dandelion Fritters

Cooking Time: 20 minutes

Servings: 4

Ingredients:

- 1 cup of dandelion petals
- 1 cup of all-purpose flour
- 1/2 cup of milk
- 1 egg
- 1 tsp of baking powder
- 1/2 tsp of salt
- Oil for frying

Instructions:

- Rinse the dandelion petals and pat dry with a paper towel.
- In a bowl, mix the flour, baking powder, and salt.
- In another bowl, beat the egg and milk together.
- Add the dry ingredients to the egg mixture and stir until smooth.
- Fold in the dandelion petals.
- Heat the oil in a frying pan over medium heat.
- Drop spoonfuls of batter into the hot oil and fry until golden brown on both sides.
- Drain on a paper towel and serve warm.

Nutritional Facts (per serving): Calories: 250, Carbs: 34g, Protein: 8g, Fat: 9g, Vitamin A: 15% of the daily value

RECIPE #7: Blackberry and Nettle Tea Cake

Cooking Time: 1 hour 15 minutes

Servings: 8

Ingredients:

- 1 cup of nettle leaves
- 1/2 cup of blackberries
- 1/2 cup of unsalted butter
- 1/2 cup of granulated sugar
- 2 eggs
- 1 1/2 cups of all-purpose flour
- 1 tsp of baking powder
- 1/4 tsp of salt
- 1/4 cup of milk

Instructions:

- Preheat the oven to 350°F (180°C).
- Rinse the nettle leaves and blanch in boiling water for 1-2 minutes.
- Drain and finely chop.
- In a bowl, cream the butter and sugar together.
- Add the eggs and beat until fluffy.
- In another bowl, mix the flour, baking powder, and salt.
- Gradually add the dry ingredients to the butter mixture, alternating with the milk.
- Fold in the chopped nettle leaves and blackberries.
- Pour the batter into a greased 8-inch (20 cm) cake pan.
- Bake for 45-50 minutes or until a toothpick inserted into the center comes clean.
- Let cool before serving.

Nutritional Facts: Calories: 310, Carbs: 38g, Protein: 5g, Fat: 16g, Vitamin A: 10% of the daily value, Vitamin C: 10% of the daily value

RECIPE #8: Pine Needle Shortbread Cookies

Cooking Time: 1 hour

Servings: 16

Ingredients:

- 2 cups of all-purpose flour
- 1 cup of unsalted butter
- 1/2 cup of granulated sugar
- 1/4 cup of pine needles
- 1/2 tsp of salt

Instructions:

- Preheat the oven to 350°F (180°C).
- Rinse the pine needles and pat dry with a paper towel.
- Finely chop the pine needles.
- In a bowl, cream the butter and sugar together.
- Add the flour, chopped pine needles, and salt to the butter mixture and stir until a dough forms.
- Roll out the dough on a floured surface to 1/2-inch (1 cm) thickness.
- Cut into shapes using cookie cutters and place them on a baking sheet lined with parchment paper.
- Bake for 10-12 minutes or until the edges turn golden brown.
- Let cool on a wire rack before serving.

Nutritional Facts: Calories: 230, Carbs: 23g, Protein: 2g, Fat: 15g, Vitamin C: 20% of the daily value

RECIPE #9: Rosehip and Apple Fruit Leather

Cooking Time: 6-8 hours

Servings: 8

Ingredients:

- 2 cups of rosehips
- 2 cups of chopped apples
- 1 cup of water
- 1/4 cup of honey

Instructions:

- Rinse the rosehips and remove the stems and seeds.
- Blend the rosehips, chopped apples, water, and honey until smooth in a blender or food processor.
- Pour the mixture into a saucepan and cook over medium heat for 10-15 minutes, stirring constantly.
- Line a baking sheet with parchment paper and pour the mixture onto it, spreading it evenly with a spatula.
- Bake in the oven at the lowest temperature for 6-8 hours or until the fruit leather is dry.
- Cut into strips and store in an airtight container.

Nutritional Facts: Calories: 70, Carbs: 19g, Protein: 1g, Fat: 0g, Vitamin C: 130% of the daily value.

RECIPE #10: Wild Violet Jelly

Cooking Time: 45 minutes

Servings: 12

Ingredients:

- 2 cups of wild violet flowers
- 4 cups of water
- 1/4 cup of lemon juice
- 1 package of powdered pectin
- 4 cups of granulated sugar

Instructions:

- Rinse the wild violet flowers and remove the stems.
- Bring the water to a boil in a saucepan and add the violet flowers.
- Simmer for 10-15 minutes and strain the liquid through a cheesecloth or fine mesh strainer.
- Combine the violet liquid, lemon juice, and pectin in another saucepan.
- Bring to a rolling boil and add the sugar, stirring constantly.
- Boil for 1 minute and remove from heat.
- Skim off any foam and pour the jelly into sterilized jars.
- Let cool before storing.

Nutritional Facts (per serving): Calories: 240, Carbs: 61g, Protein: 0g, Fat: 0g, Vitamin A: 10% of the daily value, Vitamin C: 20% of the daily value.

CHAPTER FIVE
BEVERAGES RECIPE
*

RECIPE #1: Pine Needle Tea

Cooking Time: 10-15 minutes

Servings: 2

Ingredients:

- 1 cup of fresh pine needles
- 4 cups of water
- Honey or lemon (optional)

Instructions:

- Rinse the pine needles and remove any brown parts or debris.
- In a pot, bring the water to a boil.
- Add the pine needles and let them steep for 10-15 minutes.
- Strain the tea and add honey or lemon if desired.

Serve hot.

Nutritional Facts (per serving): Calories: 0, Carbs: 0g, Protein: 0g, Fat: 0g, Vitamin C: 200% of the daily value.

RECIPE #2: Dandelion Coffee

Cooking Time: 30-45 minutes

Servings: 4

Ingredients:

- 4 cups of dandelion roots, chopped
- 4 cups of water
- Milk and sweetener (optional)

Instructions:

- Rinse and chop the dandelion roots.
- Roast the roots in the oven at 350°F for 30-45 minutes until they are dark and fragrant.
- In a pot, bring the water to a boil.
- Add the roasted dandelion roots and steep them for 5-10 minutes.
- Strain the liquid and serve with milk and sweetener if desired.

Nutritional Facts (per serving): Calories: 20, Carbs: 5g, Protein: 0g, Fat: 0g, Vitamin A: 10% of the daily value.

RECIPE #3: Elderflower Lemonade

Cooking Time: 20-25 minutes

Servings: 4

Ingredients:

- 1 cup of fresh elderflowers
- 4 cups of water
- 1 cup of lemon juice
- 1/2 cup of honey or sugar

Instructions:

- Rinse the elderflowers and remove the stems.
- In a pot, bring the water to a boil.
- Add the elderflowers and let them steep for 10-15 minutes.
- Strain the liquid and let it cool.
- Mix the elderflower tea, lemon juice, and honey/sugar in a pitcher.
- Serve over ice.

Nutritional Facts (per serving): Calories: 120, Carbs: 31g, Protein: 0g, Fat: 0g, Vitamin C: 100% of the daily value

RECIPE #4: Wild Grape Juice

Cooking Time: 1 hour

Servings: 8

Ingredients:

- 4 cups of wild grapes
- 4 cups of water
- 1/2 cup of honey or sugar

Instructions:

- Rinse the wild grapes and remove any stems or debris.
- In a pot, bring the water to a boil.
- Add the wild grapes and let them simmer for 30-40 minutes until the skins burst.
- Strain the juice through a cheesecloth or fine mesh strainer.
- Add honey or sugar to taste.
- Let cool before serving.

Nutritional Facts (per serving): Calories: 110, Carbs: 29g, Protein: 0g, Fat: 0g, Vitamin C: 15% of the daily value.

RECIPE #5: Blackberry and Mint Iced Tea

Cooking Time: 10-15 minutes

Servings: 4

Ingredients:

- 2 cups of fresh blackberries
- 4 cups of water
- 1/4 cup of honey or sugar
- 4-5 sprigs of fresh mint
- Ice

Instructions:

- Rinse the blackberries and crush them with a fork.
- In a pot, bring the water to a boil.
- Add the crushed blackberries and let them simmer for 5-10 minutes.
- Strain the liquid and let it cool.
- Mix the blackberry juice, honey/sugar, and fresh mint in a pitcher.
- Add ice and serve.

Nutritional Facts (per serving): Calories: 80, Carbs: 21g, Protein: 1g, Fat: 0g, Vitamin C: 25% of the daily value.

RECIPE #6: Chamomile Tea

Cooking Time: 5-10 minutes

Servings: 2

Ingredients:

- 1 cup of fresh chamomile flowers
- 2 cups of water
- Honey or lemon (optional)

Instructions:

- Rinse the chamomile flowers.
- In a pot, bring the water to a boil.
- Add the chamomile flowers and let them steep for 5-10 minutes.
- Strain the tea and add honey or lemon if desired.
- Serve hot or cold.

Nutritional Facts (per serving): Calories: 0, Carbs: 0g, Protein: 0g, Fat: 0g, Vitamin A: 4% of the daily value

RECIPE #7: Wild Ginger Ale

Cooking Time: 20-30 minutes

Servings: 4

Ingredients:

- 1 cup of chopped wild ginger
- 4 cups of water
- 1/2 cup of honey or sugar
- 1/4 cup of lemon juice
- 1/4 teaspoon of active dry yeast

Instructions:

- Rinse and chop the wild ginger.
- In a pot, bring the water to a boil.
- Add the wild ginger and let it simmer for 10-15 minutes.
- Strain the liquid and let it cool.
- Add honey/sugar, lemon juice, and yeast to the ginger tea.
- Stir well and let it sit for 24-48 hours until it becomes fizzy.
- Strain the mixture to remove any sediment.
- Bottle and refrigerate the ginger ale.
- Serve chilled.

Nutritional Facts (per serving): Calories: 110, Carbs: 29g, Protein: 0g, Fat: 0g, Vitamin C: 20% of the daily value.

RECIPE #8: Rosehip Tea

Cooking Time: 10-15 minutes

Servings: 2

Ingredients:

- 1 cup of fresh rosehips
- 2 cups of water
- Honey or lemon (optional)

Instructions:

- Rinse the rosehips and remove the stems and seeds.
- In a pot, bring the water to a boil.
- Add the rosehips and let them simmer for 10-15 minutes.
- Strain the tea and add honey or lemon if desired.
- Serve hot or cold.

Nutritional Facts (per serving): Calories: 0, Carbs: 0g, Protein: 0g, Fat: 0g, Vitamin C: 200% of the daily value.

RECIPE #9: Wild Mint Iced Tea

Cooking Time: 10-15 minutes

Servings: 4

Ingredients:

- 4-5 sprigs of fresh wild mint
- 4 cups of water
- 1/4 cup of honey or sugar
- Ice

Instructions:

- Rinse the wild mint.
- In a pot, bring the water to a boil.
- Add the wild mint and let it simmer for 5-10 minutes.
- Strain the liquid and let it cool.
- Mix the mint tea, honey/sugar, and ice in a pitcher.
- Serve chilled.

Nutritional Facts (per serving): Calories: 60, Carbs: 15g, Protein: 0g, Fat: 0g, Vitamin C: 10% of the daily value

RECIPE #10: Honeysuckle Lemonade

Cooking Time: 20-25 minutes

Servings:

Ingredients:

- 1 cup of honeysuckle flowers
- 1 cup of lemon juice
- 1 cup of sugar
- 8 cups of water

Instructions:

- Rinse the honeysuckle flowers and remove the green stem and sepal.
- In a large pot, bring the water to a boil.
- Add the honeysuckle flowers and let them steep for 20-25 minutes.
- Strain the liquid through a fine-mesh sieve and let it cool.
- Mix the lemon juice and sugar in a separate bowl until the sugar dissolves.
- Add the lemon mixture to the honeysuckle tea and stir well.
- Chill in the fridge for a few hours or overnight.
- Serve cold over ice.

Nutritional Facts (per serving): Calories: 140, Carbs: 36g, Protein: 0g, Fat: 0g, Vitamin C: 50% of the daily value.

Wild plants that can be eaten provide a distinctive gastronomic experience and can be a nutritious complement to any diet. To be safe, you must take precautions and confirm that the plants you are gathering are edible. One should take the required procedures to correctly identify the plants and be aware of any potential hazards before attempting to pick wild plants. By doing your research and making sure the plants you use are edible, you may confidently and securely incorporate wild plants into your repertoire of dishes.

CONCLUSION

*

Anyone interested in foraging and off-the-grid living should consult "The Complete Guide to Locating, Identifying, Harvesting, and Preparing Edible Wild Plants". This book offers a thorough reference to the vast world of wild edibles with its in-depth descriptions, vibrant images, and specific information.

Foraging has been a crucial component of our nutrition from the beginning of human history, and this book provides an interesting look at the wild foods that have kept people alive for thousands of years. Whether you're a seasoned forager or just starting out, this guide gives you all the knowledge you need to find, recognize, collect, and prepare wild plants for eating in a safe and efficient manner.

Connecting with nature and the land is among foraging's most important advantages. We may better comprehend the connectivity of all living things and the crucial function that wild edibles serve in our ecosystem by learning about and engaging with the natural world around us.

This guide covers a variety of wild delicacies, such as fruits, nuts, roots, shoots, and leaves, and offers thorough details on their nutritional value, therapeutic benefits, and culinary applications. In order to ensure that readers can make use of the many advantages of foraging while safeguarding and preserving our natural environment, it also contains helpful tips on foraging ethics, safety, and sustainability.

This guide provides recipes for employing wild edibles in numerous delectable and healthful dishes, in addition to thorough descriptions and images of the plants. These recipes provide a multitude of inventive and delectable ways to use wild plants in your diet, ranging from spicy soups and stews to sweet sweets and preserves.

For anyone interested in foraging and off-the-grid living, "The Complete Guide to Locating, Identifying, Harvesting, and Preparing Edible Wild Plants" is a thorough and useful reference. This guide provides a wealth of knowledge, insights, and inspiration for discovering the abundant world of wild foods, whether you are an experienced forager or just starting out. So go outside and find the numerous tasty and healthy wild plants that are ready to be appreciated!

Download your bonus by scanning the QR code.

No email is required.

Thank you for your purchase.

I would be very pleased if you would leave an honest review on Amazon.

Made in the USA
Las Vegas, NV
07 June 2023

73110794R00059